Jewish
Pioneers
of
New Mexico

Jewish Pioneers
of
New Mexico

Foreword
by Thomas E. Chávez

Main text compiled and edited
by Tomas Jaehn

With an Afterword
by Henry J. Tobias

MUSEUM OF NEW MEXICO PRESS

SANTA FE

Jacket and cover illustrations:

front flap: **Hugo Aaron Zeckendorf, c. 1866** (page 73).

front cover, left: **Bertha Staab Nordhaus, c. 1895** (page 79);

front cover, right: **Solomon Jacob Spiegelberg, ca. 1856.**
Oil on canvas by Constance Mayer, courtesy of the Palace of the Governors.

Spiegelberg was New Mexico's first known German-Jewish immigrant.
Museum of New Mexico; gift of Ann S. Brown and Frederick Spiegelberg.

back cover, left: **Helenita Zeckendorf, c. 1874** (page 72);

back cover, right: **Charles Ilfeld** (page 32).

Based on the exhibition "Jewish Pioneers of New Mexico, 1821–1917," at the Palace of Governors, Museum of New Mexico, Santa Fe, October 2000–December 2004.

Project editor: Mary Wachs
Copy editor: Heidi Utz
Manuscript typist and proofreader: Joan Chernock
Design and production: Bruce Taylor Hamilton
Based upon the exhibition design by Susan Hyde Holmes
Maps: Deborah Reade
Studio photography by Blair Clark
Composition: Set in Centaur
Manufactured in Singapore

Library of Congress Cataloging-in-Publication Data

Jaehn, Tomas.
    Jewish pioneers of New Mexico / foreword by Thomas E. Chávez ; main text compiled and edited by Tomás Jaehn; with an afterword by Henry J. Tobias.—1st ed.
Based on the exhibition "Jewish Pioneers of New Mexico, 1821–1917," at
the Palace of the Governors, Museum of New Mexico.
ISBN 0-89013-466-9 (alk. paper)—ISBN 0-89013-467-7 (Pbk : alk. paper)
    1. Jews—New Mexico—History. 2. Jews—New Mexico--History—Pictorial works.
3. Jews, European—New Mexico—History—Pictorial works. 4. Ashkenazim—New Mexico
—History—Pictorial works.
I. Museum of New Mexico. II. Title.
    F805.J5J34 2003
    978.9'004924--dc22
                                                                    2003015632

Museum of New Mexico Press
Post Office Box 2087
Santa Fe, New Mexico 87504

Contents

Foreword

There is something special about New Mexico's history because the place is, as one early governor described it, "remote beyond compare," or more aptly, landlocked and distant from seacoasts, it has always been sparsely populated. This combination of distance and small population has preserved a clearer view of its history. New Mexico's heritage has not been obscured by an overwhelming population growth with its incumbent development. Yesteryears' people and cultural vestiges have not been buried by an influx of new residents, urbanization, and sprawl. Instead, the state retains its sense of existing in a continuum, as historical connections remain obvious today.

For many reasons, the nineteenth century was a pivotal time in New Mexico's history. The area—roughly defined as the current state boundaries, plus El Paso and southern Colorado, with the Rio Grande and its tributaries serving as a focal point—was a part of the vice regency of New Spain in the Spanish Empire. It then became a department in the newly formed independent country of Mexico and ended the century as a U.S. territory. New Mexico progressed from a closed, border-defensive frontier to a free-trade port of entry and, finally, to an integral piece in the American expansionist scheme of Manifest Destiny.

At the same time, European history evolved to converge with New Mexico's, leading to the legacy of the Jewish pioneers. The first wave of Jewish immigrants into the state took place in the 1840s and 1850s. Most of these Ashkenazi Jews originated in the German states, with the rest from eastern Europe and Russia. They were the first Jews in New Mexico to acknowledge their religion.

These initial immigrants were a product of a larger emigration to the Americas due to political, economic, and social events in eighteenth- and nineteenth-century Europe. Along with an almost-constant state of war, a climate of economic depression, nationalism, social restriction, and anti-Semitism had replaced the Enlightenment's optimism.

With the failure of the last gasp of the liberal revolutions and republican governments in the 1840s, a large migration left Europe for the United States. The immigrants sailed across the Atlantic Ocean for the eastern shore of a country not even seventy-five years old, a place in which they believed the ideas of the Enlightenment still existed. There, in such cities as Baltimore, New York, and Philadelphia, most of them began their American lives in new urban environs.

A few more adventurous young immigrants decided to follow the lure of the West. The new country of Mexico had opened its borders to international trade, giving rise to the Santa Fe Trail. The Trail stretched from Missouri across the Great Plains and into northern Mexico, where it connected with the long-established Chihuahua Trail at the more than two centuries old village of Santa Fe. This new commercial route quickly became legendary for its economic opportunities. And for more than a few merchants and traders, Mexico's northern department and its capital of Santa Fe seemed an ideal location in which to begin anew.

New Mexico was settled by Spain in 1598. Santa Fe, founded as early as 1607, became the capital in 1610. After Mexican independence in 1821, New Mexico was perfectly situated to become an international port of entry. Santa Fe was a little more than 800 miles of relatively flat terrain away from the western settlements of the United States, which, after the U.S. acquired the Louisiana Territory, extended to the Arkansas River, just northeast of New Mexico.

The international commerce enabled by the Santa Fe Trail was a perfect complement for both the United States and Mexico. New Mexico became the "middle man" of the trade, and within the first twenty years of the Trail's opening, many men from both the United States and Mexico had realized success.

Some of the early men to enter New Mexico after Mexican independence, in the 1820s and 1830s, have been identified as Jews. They came as fur trappers or as members of merchant caravans to trade in Mexico, and participated in Jacksonian America's larger scheme of enterprise. However, while pioneers in their own right, none of these first individuals remained in New Mexico.

The first Jewish men to stay in the Territory arrived in the 1840s. These mostly young, single men from the German states immediately participated in society and eventually began families. They sought greater opportunity in New Mexico's sparse, small settlements and often found it.

These men opened stores usually on the main plaza in towns along the commercial routes, served as quartermasters and sutlers for the U.S. Army, traded, and became involved with various Indian tribes. They were quick to integrate themselves into society, where social and cultural institutions provided order to the growing Anglo population.

Such active participation in civic life soon evolved into political service. By 1890 Jewish men had served in many of the elective offices of the Territory. They actively sought to contribute to their new homes because, unlike many immigrants elsewhere, they were welcomed into the community and thus, able to achieve respect and influence.

By the time New Mexico became a state in 1912, the Jewish community had become fully integrated into New Mexican society. Their temples stood as testimonials to their faith, and their participation in and support for education, music, arts, history, and even volunteer fire departments and tree-planting campaigns expressed their willingness to work with others to improve the whole. They became leaders in New Mexico's social and civic life.

Immigration to New Mexico and the United States was disrupted by World War I and ended in 1924. New Mexico had ceased to be a frontier attraction. But the legacy of New Mexico's pioneer Jews continues. The great tapestry of New Mexico's heritage owes much of its attraction to the lives of its pioneer Jews.

—Thomas E. Chávez

Acknowledgments

Jewish Pioneers of New Mexico is based on the exhibition "Jewish Pioneers of New Mexico, 1821–1917," conceived and organized by guest curators Felix and Susan Warburg and curator David Snow for the Palace of the Governors in Santa Fe, New Mexico. The exhibition and, to a large extent, this book represent the collaborative work of many participants and contributors, too numerous to thank individually. The Palace of the Governors acknowledges the many lenders of artifacts who made this exhibition possible. A special thank you is extended to all the members of the Exhibition Committee. This committee, along with the Academic Committee of Mary Jean Cook, Claire Grossman, Stan Hordes, Sharon Niederman, Henry J. Tobias, Felix Warburg, and Susan Warburg, spent long hours to make "Jewish Pioneers of New Mexico" an interesting and, it is hoped, historically accurate work. Thank you to Kate Hogue, Registrar, and Lou Ann Shurbert, former educator, for their care and attention to locating and returning many of the valuable items borrowed for this show and book. With regard to this publication, thank you to Frances Levine, director of the Palace of the Governors, who was a persistent and knowledgeable supporter of this project, to Blair Clark for his fine photographic work, and to Mary Wachs, editorial director at the Museum of New Mexico Press, who skillfully guided the editorial and design process of this book.

Financial support is crucial to all successful exhibitions, and this one is no exception. Many, many people and organizations, too numerous to mention individually, made generous financial contributions to this endeavor. Some of the major contributors were Wells Fargo Bank; La Fonda Hotel; Sam and Ethel Ballen; Barbara and Eric Dobkin; the Albert and Ethel Herzstein Charitable Foundation; Emily Fisher Landau; the Max and Anna Levinson Foundation; Carol Prius and John Hart, the Jessica Fund; the Seligman Foundation; and the Zeckendorf Foundation. To all of the contributors, thank you very, very much.

Finally, beyond the financial and curatorial work for this exhibition, thanks must go to Tom Chávez, former director of the Palace of the Governors; David Snow, former curator at the Palace of the Governors; and again, Susan and Felix Warburg of San Francisco, without whose energy and dedication this fine exhibition and this book would not have been possible.

—Tomas Jaehn
Librarian, Fray Angélico Chávez Library,
Palace of the Governors

Introduction

Jewish Pioneers of New Mexico tells the story of the first openly practicing Jews who came to New Mexico in the nineteenth and early twentieth centuries. As these new immigrants settled in the region and made it their home, their personal stories became interwoven with the history of the state. Their legacy is alive today throughout New Mexico and the greater West, where their descendants continue to carry their names.

Until now, the history of New Mexico's Jewish pioneers has been scattered in fragments of letters, diaries, memoirs, and family stories, remaining largely untold. This book, along with its related exhibition, attempts to connect the many pieces into a cohesive whole, while casting light on the immense contributions of these pioneers to the state's cultural, civic, economic, and creative life.

Historians believe that Spanish and Portuguese Sephardic Jews participated in the first exploration and settlement efforts in New Mexico in the early seventeenth century. During a period of religious cleansing by the Iberian monarchies in the late fifteenth century, their ancestors converted to Catholicism. To evade the Holy Office of the Inquisition's rage, they outwardly appeared Catholic while privately maintaining their Jewish identities and passing them on to their descendants. These *Conversos,* while of significant interest to historians, are beyond the scope of this study and will not be discussed. Instead, this book concentrates on the emigration of Ashkenazi Jews from Germany and Central Europe, beginning with the opening of the Santa Fe Trail in 1821 and the subsequent United States occupation of the territory, and ending in the early twentieth century.

The Museum's work focuses on the legacies of these pioneers, with extensive and diligent research among records available to curators and consultants. Yet history is never definitive, nor is historical research ever complete. It is our hope that this book will stimulate future study and research of this pioneer era. The curators at the Palace of the Governors Museum have defined the term *pioneer* broadly here, to encompass the varied experiences of these early Jewish immigrants. Included among the pioneers are those who were first to arrive, those who initially moved into rural areas or who lived among American Indian communities, those who were forerunners in helping to establish community institutions, and those who were first to form religious congregations. These achievements helped build New Mexico's patrimony, and all who participated were pioneers.

Chapter One *Immigration*

During the first half of the nineteenth century, the United States purchased Louisiana, expanded into the Pacific Northwest, and added the northern half of Mexico. The Santa Fe Trail became a trade route from the eastern states to the newly acquired western territories. The Oregon and Old Spanish Trails led to the West Coast, and the Chihuahua Trail (Camino Real) connected New Mexico to Mexico. The spirit of Manifest Destiny—the publicly sanctioned westward drive to populate the continent—prevailed, and many adventurous people set out to make their fortune, and, in some cases, establish new homes and become a part of a new land. Many young Jewish immigrants arriving from the German states joined in this movement. Westport, Kansas, and Independence and St. Joseph, Missouri, were the last cities they saw before they headed west via the Santa Fe Trail.

The first wave of northern European Jewish immigrants to New Mexico arrived in the 1840s and 1850s, primarily from the region today known as Germany. Other Jewish pioneers may have crossed the Santa Fe Trail and entered New Mexico earlier, but these men did not settle in New Mexico. Because of political, economic, and social events in western Europe between 1750 and 1850, the first half of the nineteenth century saw a marked increase in the number of German Jews who came to America and its western territories.

A second wave of Jewish immigrants coincided with the arrival of the railroad in New Mexico. In April 1879 the first train of the Atchison, Topeka, and Santa Fe Railway rolled into Las Vegas, New Mexico. Nearly one-third of the total rail mileage in the state was built within the brief period from 1879 to 1881. By 1881 the AT&SF had extended west into Arizona, on its way to Los Angeles and south to El Paso, where it connected with the Southern Pacific Railroad. The railroad supplanted the Santa Fe Trail and its mule-powered wagons, and since Santa Fe was not a stop along the new rail route, New Mexico's capital for already more than 250 years lost some of its importance.

1830–1849 Arrivals

Appel, Nathan Benjamin, *b. Hochstadt, Germany*
Beuthner brothers
Frankfort, Jacob
Freudenthal brothers (Phoebus, Julius)
Gold, Louis, *b. Poland*
Goldstein brothers
Kahn, Louis
Katz, Bernard
Latz, Bernard, *b. Posen, Prussian Poland*
Lewatsy [sic Lewatsky]
Rosenstein, Simon
Spiegelberg (Levi, Solomon Jacob),
   b. Natzungen, Westphalia, Germany

1850–1869 Arrivals

Amberg brothers (Jacob, Moses), *b. Arnsberg, Germany*
   (suburb of Heidelberg)
Bibo brothers (Joseph, Samson, Solomon), *b. Bräkel,*
   Warburg, Germany
Biernbaum brothers
Bloomfield, Morris
Brunswick, Marcus
Calisch, Theodore
De Leon, David, *b. South Carolina*
Dittenhoffer brothers (Sam, A.B.), *b. New York City*
Eldot brothers (Sam, Nathan)
Elsberg brothers (Albert, Gustave)
Felsenthal, Louis, *b. Iserlohn, Westphalia, Germany*
Hecht, Ben
Hersch, Joseph, *b. Poland*
Ilfeld brothers (Charles, Louis, Noa, Herman)
Jaffa brothers (Solomon, Henry, Samud), *b. Hesse*
   Kassel, Germany
Kahn, Isaac
Kihlberg, Frank
Kirchner, August, *b. Hanover, Germany*
Lesinsky brothers (Morris, Charles, Henry),
   b. Prussian Poland
Letcher, Adolf
Lowenstein, Benjamin, *b. Bavaria, Germany*
Lowitsky, M.
Mears, Otto, *b. Kurland, Latvia*
Morrison, Arthur
Neustadt brothers (Samuel, Charles, Simon)
Nussbaum, Jacob
Obermayer, Herman, *b. Kriegshaber, Bavaria*
Price brothers
Probst, Charles, *b. Hanover, Germany*
Rosenbaum, Louis
(continues on page 3)

The railroad heralded a new period of economic activity and social upheaval. Businesses expanded and diversified. New people arrived in greater numbers and formed communities that included Clayton, Wagon Mound, Roswell, Mountainair, Tucumcari, and Deming to serve the railroad. Older towns, such as Las Vegas and Albuquerque, changed and grew, becoming state economic centers.

In broad terms, the Jewish population of New Mexico expanded proportionally with the general population, from less than 200 people by 1880 to more than 400 at the turn of the century. Jewish women notably were missing during the early period of immigration. In 1860 New Mexico could count two "Hebrew ladies," both the wives of Spiegelberg men. As Las Vegas and Albuquerque grew, so did their Jewish populations, quickly surpassing that of Santa Fe.

The demographics of the Jewish citizens also changed. Earlier pioneers had aged or moved out of New Mexico. Although half of the original Jewish pioneers had left New Mexico by 1880, the Jewish population in the state proceeded to double by the end of the century. In 1893 the last member of the Spiegelberg family left New Mexico after fifty years of business in the area. Some moved back east or returned to Europe; others continued west to Arizona and California.

Continuing the trend that began in the 1880s and paralleling immigration patterns elsewhere, the new Jewish immigrants reflected eastern European origins. Russian, Polish, Lithuanian, and Romanian Jews joined earlier German immigrants in New Mexico. The number of native-born Jews grew with the passage of time. In 1912 New Mexico became the forty-seventh state in the Union, and subsequent generations of New Mexican Jews began to identify themselves as American rather than European. New Mexico's largest city, Albuquerque, began its rise as the state's urban and commercial center, and in time became the heart and center of New Mexico's Jewish population.

In 1924 national laws restricting immigration came into effect, resulting in a dramatic drop both in national and New Mexican immigration figures. The arrival of foreign-born Jewish settlers virtually ended, and the state's days as a frontier attraction to young Jewish men and women seeking freedom and opportunity had ended.

Until then, it was the freedom, hope, and economic opportunity, spread by European philosophers, that attracted Jewish men and women to consider making their new homes in the United States in general, and New Mexico and the West in particular. The Age of Enlightenment, with its embrace of the social contract promulgated by philosophers Jean-Jacques Rousseau, François Voltaire, John Locke, and Denis Diderot, catalyzed the American and French Revolutions. The cry for Liberty, Equality, and Brotherhood gave hope to Europe's Jewish population.

As the reviewer of a recent publication on the history of Jews in Germany poignantly phrased it, the Jewish citizens "could taste the Enlightenment, they fairly quivered in anticipation of all it had to offer, yet they could not get close enough to taste." The Jews' spirit of optimism continued with the rise of Napoleon. France and countries it occupied, as well as German kingdoms and principalities like Prussia and Baden, granted Jews citizenship, equal education, surnames, suffrage, and also the right to engage in previously forbidden professions. For instance, in 1812 a Baron Von Spegelberg reputedly rewarded Jacob Spiegelberg's father for his trustworthiness and reliability in managing his estate by giving him his surname under the Code of Napoleon.

Napoleon's 1815 defeat at Waterloo, however, led to the revocation of many recently granted rights. The Jews, particularly in the German states, felt this loss bitterly. Once again they were subjected to economic and social restrictions. The concept of an all-Christian Teutonic state led to debates on the role of the Jew. It was this climate of economic depression, nationalism, social restriction, and anti-Semitism (in part caused by the reaction to the liberal revolutions of the 1840s that arose across Europe) that made German Jews search for places to immigrate. Because they sought greater individual and social freedom, as well as equal opportunity, the young United States attracted many.

During the time of the German mass immigration, the prospect of freedom and a future were frequently advertised in many publications, including travel descriptions, emigration guidebooks, prospectuses and brochures, enticing and frightening stories, and pamphlets and song sheets. Some Jewish immigrants chose to move to the American West, where settlements were sparse and opportunities seemed greater than in the already-crowded immigrant quarters of

Rosenwald brothers (Emanuel, Joseph), *b. Dittenhofen, Germany*
Sach brothers
Scheurich, Aloys
Schultz brothers (S., Aron)
Schultz brothers (Joseph, Max)
Schuster, Benjamin
Schwartzkopf brothers (Maurice, Phillip)
Seligman brothers (Bernard, Adolf, Sigmund), *b. Bayersdorf, Bavaria, Germany*
Spiegelberg brothers, *b. Natzungen, Westphalia, Germany*
Spiegelberg, Abraham, *b. New York, NY*
Staab brothers (Abraham, Zadoc), *b. Lüdge, Hesse Kassel, Hanover, Germany*
Stern brothers (Isadore, Leon B.)
Sulzbacher, Louis
Wedeles, Simon
Weinheim, Selig
Zeckendorf brothers (Aaron, Louis, William), *b. Hemmendorf, Hanover, Germany*

1870–1879 Arrivals

Abraham, David, *b. Poland (original name: Dobrzinsky)*
Bacharach
Back brothers
Barth, Solomon
Cohen, Isaac, *b. Jerusalem*
Eiseman brothers (Albert, Nathan, and others), *b. Mossbach, Germany*
Friedman
Gellermann
Grant brothers, *b. Blodslavicz, Poland*
Grunsfeld brothers (Alfred, Albert, Ernest), *b. Erfurt, Germany*
Gusdorf brothers (Alexander, Gerson), *b. Pyrmont, Westphalia, Germany*
Guttman
Harberg, Carl
Hays, May
Kohn, Samuel, *b. Pilsen, Germany*
Levy, Julius E.
Levy, Thomas
May, Jonn
Regensberg brothers (Jacob, ?), *b. Hesse Cassel, Germany*
Salsbury, John Seixas, *b. New York*
Trauer, Maurice
Vorenberg brothers
Waxman
Weisl, Bernard
Winternitz, David, *b. Prague, Czechoslovakia (Austrian Empire)*

Eastern cities. The Jewish population of New Mexico during the 1850s and 1860s comprised both northern and central European immigrants, with the majority from Germany.

The young men who entered New Mexico in the mid- and late-1800s frequently worked as merchants and clerks. Though some came from wealthy backgrounds, many were from less affluent families whose lives and fortunes were difficult. The records of the Lilienfeld, Spiegelberg, and Zeckendorf families in Germany, for instance, list the men as street vendors, peddlers, tradesmen, or shoemakers, or as unemployed. Once established and seeking companionship, some returned briefly to the East Coast or Europe to get married, and then bring their brides to New Mexico. Others married local Anglo, Hispanic, or Native American women.

By the 1860s Jewish families began to form in New Mexico, and not surprisingly, many of them were related. Quite often they came from the same region in Germany or, like the Gusdorf and Ilfeld families, were linked through a complex web of intermarriage in their homeland. First were the brothers, such as the Spiegelbergs, Seligmans, and Staabs, of Santa Fe; the Zeckendorfs of Albuquerque; the Beuthners of Taos; and the Birnbaums of Mora. Many were cousins, and often their marriages connected the families even more tightly. Unions between several brothers of one family and several sisters of another family were not uncommon.

For instance, Betti Lilienfeld and her family came from the town of Kirchrode, now a part of Hannover. She married Jacob Spiegelberg, and their eldest son was Solomon Jacob Spiegelberg, who became the first known German-Jewish merchant to settle in Santa Fe, arriving in 1844. His five brothers followed to join him in a mercantile business on the Plaza, with the youngest, Willi, arriving in 1859. He and his brother Lehman ran the family firm until the 1890s. Brother Levi Spiegelberg acted as their New York agent, while Solomon handled their German interests in Frankfurt. Additionally, after Betti Lilienfeld's sister, Johanna, married Abraham Zeckendorf, they became parents to Aaron, Louis, and William, who immigrated to New Mexico and Arizona. Mina Lilienfeld's son-in-law, Philip Drachman, moved to Arizona, where he became a business partner with the Zeckendorfs. Such interwoven family relationships, leading to close business relationships, created strong social, religious, and economic ties that served them well in their new country.

While strong family bonds eased one's cultural integration into a new country, a good education and social skills added to the promise of success. Willi Spiegelberg, for instance, spoke German, Spanish, and English, and may have even learned some Indian languages; he was also known for his skills with a lariat and whip. He cofounded and acted as treasurer of the Second National Bank of New Mexico, was appointed probate judge of Santa Fe County in 1884, and served as mayor of Santa Fe in the 1880s. He also was active as a Freemason and Germania Club member. In 1874 Willi married American-born Flora Langerman, in Nuremberg, Germany. After a yearlong honeymoon in Europe, he brought her back to Santa Fe, where Flora gave birth to their daughters, Betty and Rose. Perhaps inspired by Lehman and his wife, Betty, Willi liquidated the "House of Spiegelberg" in the early 1890s and moved his wife and daughters to New York for its educational, social, and religious opportunities. Flora Spiegelberg brought accomplishments of her own to the New Mexico frontier. Archbishop Jean Baptiste Lamy admired her musical and linguistic abilities, especially since he had a hard time finding locals who could converse with him in French. Hearing of her interest in botany and gardening, the archbishop in 1879 planted two willow trees in the front yard of her new Santa Fe home at 237 East Palace Avenue.

Many of the first Jewish pioneers came from what today is Germany. Several of these pioneer families were already related before they migrated to New Mexico. For example, the Spiegelberg, Zeckendorf, and Staab families, as well as the Gusdorf and Ilfeld families, were related in a complex web of intermarriage in Germany.

Willi Spiegelberg's Engagement Photograph
1873

Willi Spiegelberg, the youngest of the six brothers, arrived in Santa Fe in 1859 to join his brothers in their mercantile business on the Plaza. Willi and his brother Lehman ran the family mercantile firm until the 1890s. Their brother Levi acted as their agent in New York, and their brother Solomon Jacob handled their interests in Frankfurt, Germany.

Willi spoke German, Spanish, English, and four Indian dialects, and he was known as an expert with both lariat and whip. He became treasurer of the Second National Bank of New Mexico, was appointed probate judge of Santa Fe County in 1884, and served as mayor of Santa Fe. He also was active in both the Masons and the Germania Club.

In 1874 Willi married American-born Flora Langerman in Nuremberg. After a one-year honeymoon in Europe, he brought her to Santa Fe, where their daughters, Betty and Rose, were born.

Willi liquidated the "House of Spiegelberg" in the early 1890s, and moved his wife and daughters to New York, where he felt there were better educational, social, and religious opportunities for his family. Lehman and his wife, Betty, had already moved there, for similar reasons.

Courtesy Felix and Susan (Spiegelberg) Warburg, San Francisco, California

Flora Langerman Spiegelberg, Age Sixteen
1873

Flora was a striking redhead when she and Willi Spiegelberg became engaged in 1873, in Nuremberg. She was born in New York in 1857, but upon the death of her father, William Langerman, her mother, Rosalia, decided to return to her German family with her children.

Flora was well educated for her time. At sixteen she spoke fluent English, German, and French, and had studied Latin and history. She embroidered, gardened, and played the piano.

She brought these accomplishments with her to the New Mexico frontier. Archbishop Jean Baptiste Lamy admired her musical and linguistic proficiencies; it was difficult to find someone who could converse with him in French. Learning of her interest in botany and gardening, the archbishop personally planted two willow trees in front of her new house at 237 East Palace Avenue, in 1879. Flora and Willi also had a close friendship with Governor Lew Wallace, who was writing *Ben Hur* while living in the Palace of the Governors. Her intellectual curiosity and cosmopolitan aura made Flora one of Santa Fe's social leaders. She was also a community leader through her active concerns for education, religion, and other civic needs.

Courtesy Felix and Susan (Spiegelberg) Warburg, San Francisco, California

Betti Lilienfeld

c. 1850

Betti Lilienfeld married Jacob Spiegelberg and was the mother of their ten children: Solomon Jacob, Levi, Eva, Abraham, Elias, Hannchen, Emanuel, Mindelchen, Lehman, and Wolf (Willi).

Her sister and a niece also married into prominent Jewish families, namely the Zeckendorfs and Drachmans, who became leading Jewish merchants in New Mexico and then in Tucson, Arizona.

Courtesy Leopold and Emma Adler II, Savannah, Georgia

Jacob Spiegelberg

c. 1850, Westphalia, Germany

Patriarch of the "Santa Fe Spiegelberg brothers," Jacob Spiegelberg supported his family as a street vendor, peddler, and tradesman.

According to family history, Jacob's father received the name "Spiegelberg" in 1812 under the Code of Napoleon from a Baron Von Speigelberg, whose estate he managed, and who found him to be trustworthy and reliable.

Courtesy Leopold and Emma Adler II, Savannah, Georgia

The Spiegelberg Brothers

c. 1865–70

left to right: Willi, Emmanuel, Solomon Jacob, Levi, and Lehman. These brothers formed one of the largest commercial firms in Santa Fe.

Museum of New Mexico, Neg. No. 11025

The Zeckendorfs

The Zeckendorf family traces its roots to Spain. In the wake of the Inquisition, the family fled to Holland. Later they moved to Zeckendorf, Germany, and eventually settled in the village of Hemmendorf. Aaron Zeckendorf, eldest son of a shoemaker in Hannover and grandson of a rabbi, arrived in New Mexico in 1854, at age eighteen. There, he clerked for his Spiegelberg cousins, who then backed him when he opened his own store in Santa Fe a year later. He had help from his younger brothers Louis and William when he opened branches in Albuquerque and Rio Mimbres (Deming). William enlisted in the Union Army in 1862.

After weathering the ups and downs of business, the brothers decided to try and make a go of it elsewhere. In 1866 Louis left Albuquerque with twelve wagonloads of goods for Tucson, where he found success. After transporting goods between the two cities for some time, he eventually diversified the business into government contracts. The brothers operated mail routes and became suppliers to military posts and Indian reservations.

Louis moved to New York City in 1869, where, as resident buyer, he had an advantage in contracts and commodities bidding, further improving the family business. The Zeckendorfs went on to pursue interests in real estate, mining, and lumber. William became involved in Arizona politics and represented Pima County in the Arizona Territorial Legislature. By 1870 the Zeckendorfs had left New Mexico and made Arizona their headquarters.

Louis Zeckendorf
n.d.

Louis was Aaron Zeckendorf's business partner. In 1869 Louis moved to New York, where he represented the family firm as resident buyer, thereby strengthening the business.

Courtesy Arizona Historical Society Library

William Zeckendorf
c. 1875

Soon after arriving in New Mexico, William Zeckendorf served as a volunteer Union soldier during the Civil War. In 1868 his brothers sent him to Tucson, Arizona, to manage the Zeckendorf branch store. In 1875 he was elected to the Arizona Territorial Legislature from Pima County.

Courtesy Arizona Historical Society

background:

The Zeckendorf House

1960

This house (no. 24) was owned by three generations of Zeckendorfs—Solomon, son Abraham, and grandson Karl—from 1856 until 1938.

Courtesy Bettina Lyons (Zeckendorf), Tucson, Arizona

The Zeckendorf Women

1864

From left to right are Lea Lilienfeld, Julia Zeckendorf, Johanna Lilienfeld Zeckendorf, and young Frieda Steinfeld. These four women were left behind in Hemmendorf, Germany, after the Zeckendorf children had emigrated to America. Partings were sad affairs because mothers never knew if they would see their children again, so they exchanged photographs. In this case there was a happy ending: Louis Zeckendorf became wealthy enough to return to Germany in 1866.

Courtesy Arizona Historical Society Library

The Staabs

The two Staab brothers were born in Lüdge, Westphalia, Germany: Zadoc in 1835, and Abraham in 1839. In 1853 Zadoc arrived in Santa Fe, where he found work with his Spiegelberg cousins, as did his brother. In 1859 the Staabs opened their own retail store in Santa Fe and became post traders to Fort Marcy. Zadoc then moved to New York City to become the resident buyer.

By 1871 Z. Staab & Bro. was in the wholesale business, serving New Mexico Territory as well as Texas, Mexico, Arizona, and southern Colorado. They manufactured their own clothing and shoes in the East, and while Abraham minded the store in Santa Fe, Zadoc made annual buying trips to Europe.

In the words of Abraham Staab's granddaughter, Elizabeth Nordhaus Minces, in *The Family: Early Days in New Mexico*:

> *Like many of the other German Jews,* [my grandfather] *came West to find a new life after hearing stories of gold and of opportunities for trade in fur, wool and sheep, and other merchandise. They had left Europe to escape military conscription and life in the ghetto. In the West they came as merchant peddlers, as sutlers to the Army, or they started small stores and posts on Indian reservations, expanding their trade throughout New Mexico, including what is now parts of Colorado, Arizona, and as far south as Durango and Chihuahua in Mexico. Many of the merchants flourished, and as they grew and needed experienced help, they brought brothers, nephews and cousins to work for them.*
>
> *. . . Grandfather was one of the founders and first president of the Santa Fe Chamber of Commerce, a director of the First National Bank in Santa Fe, a member of the Board of County Commissioners, and secretary of the First Capitol Building Commission.*
>
> *There was a so-called 'Santa Fe Ring' in politics, headed by Thomas Benton Catron, and with the aid of various stalwart individuals in the Republican Party, Catron became the most dominant politician and business figure ever to hold sway in New Mexico. . . . The original ring included A. Staab, Robert Lorivll, Frank W. Springer and H. L. Waldo.*
>
> *One story told by my mother* [Bertha Staab Nordhaus] *was that whenever Grandfather played poker there would always be a 20 dollar gold piece at the plate of each child the next morning. Was that to convince Grandmother that he always won?*

Abraham Staab

n.d.

A Santa Fe Booster and power broker, Staab fought to keep the capital in Santa Fe and to bring the railroad to town.

Museum of New Mexico, Neg. No. 11040

Mr. Staab [opposite] was disappointed when the Santa Fe Railroad did not build their main line through Santa Fe but built only a spur from Lamy to Santa Fe. The following year he headed a group of businessmen who contacted the officials of the Denver & Rio Grande Railroad (a narrow-gauge) about coming to Santa Fe. The Santa Fe Railroad gave the 1881 Territorial legislators passes to Denver to meet with the Denver & Rio Grande directors in order to stimulate their interest. Mr. Staab paid all the other expenses of the trip and gave each a top hat with a gold-headed cane in addition. Their efforts were successful and in 1889 the Denver and Rio Grande Railroad line from Denver came into Santa Fe.

—Beatrice Ilfeld Meyer,
Don Luis Ilfeld: Memories of His Daughter

above:
Merchants on the Santa Fe Trail
c. 1870

Left to right: Bernard Seligman, Zadoc Staab, Lehman Spiegelberg, and Kiowa Indians
Museum of New Mexico, Neg. No. 7890

background:
Santa Fe Plaza, Southeast Corner
c. 1855

The southeast corner of the plaza in Santa Fe, showing the Exchange Hotel (later La Fonda) on the left and the firm of Seligman & Clever on the right.
Museum of New Mexico, Neg. No. 10685

Colt Revolver

Early twentieth century

This .38-caliber Colt revolver was the personal property of Solomon Bibo. He used it at his store in San Rafael and at the sheep camp, mostly for protection.

Courtesy Saul Cohen, Santa Fe

Trunk

Nineteenth century

Solomon Spiegelberg, a first cousin of the five Spiegelberg brothers, traveled the Santa Fe Trail by covered wagon. With his wife, Bertha, they brought some of their possessions in this trunk. The leather trunk was patented in 1865.

Palace of the Governors Collections (11391/45, 11390/45)

Cordial Liqueur Chest

Nineteenth century

This heirloom chest was given to Isaac Bibo, patriarch of the Bibo clan, for fifty years of service in the Jewish elementary schools in Europe. The inscription reads, "To Their Friend Bibo for His 50th Anniversary Dedicated by Hasse, Lorenz, Wagner."

Courtesy Milton & Julia Seligman, Albuquerque

It was in 1867 that I left New York City for the West. I arrived in St. Louis July 16 of that year. . . . When I resumed my westward journey, I boarded a car which was attached to what seemed a work or construction train carrying regular freight, bridge material and other heavy material for road construction. The car contained plain wooden benches and the cushion I provided by rolling up my overcoat and blanket. . . .

—Nathan Bibo,
Reminiscences of Early New Mexico

Charles Ilfeld

c. 1870

Arriving in Santa Fe in 1865 at age eighteen, Charles Ilfeld came to the United States to escape Prussian conscription. He arrived with five dollars in his pocket and went on to build a mercantile empire in the Southwest.

Museum of New Mexico, Neg. No. 70674

The Ilfelds

Charles Ilfeld, the patriarch of this pioneering merchant family, arrived in New Mexico from his home in Homburg Von der Höhe, Germany, in 1865. He was preceded by an older brother, Herman, who was then in partnership with the mercantile firm of Elsberg and Amberg in Santa Fe. Charles was recruited by his brother as their agent in Taos. By 1867 he had formed a partnership with the respected Jewish trader Adolph Letcher in Taos. Perceiving that Las Vegas might promote a lucrative business venture, the two merchants loaded their goods on seventy-five burros and made their way to that boomtown.

Charles sent for his younger brothers over the next several years, trained them in his business, and encouraged them, often with start-up funds, to open their own mercantile businesses. In 1874 Charles bought out his partner and returned to Germany, where he married Adele Nordhaus. Accompanying them on their return to Las Vegas was her brother, Max, who eventually became president of the Ilfeld Company. The younger Ilfeld brothers married the daughters of other prominent Jewish merchants in Northern New Mexico: Staab, Goldberg, Salsbury, Schutz, Spiegelberg, and Baer. The extended Ilfeld family maintained an active religious and social prominence well into the twentieth century.

Places in New Mexico with a Jewish Presence, 1850–1900
(Excluding Santa Fe, Albuquerque, and Las Vegas)

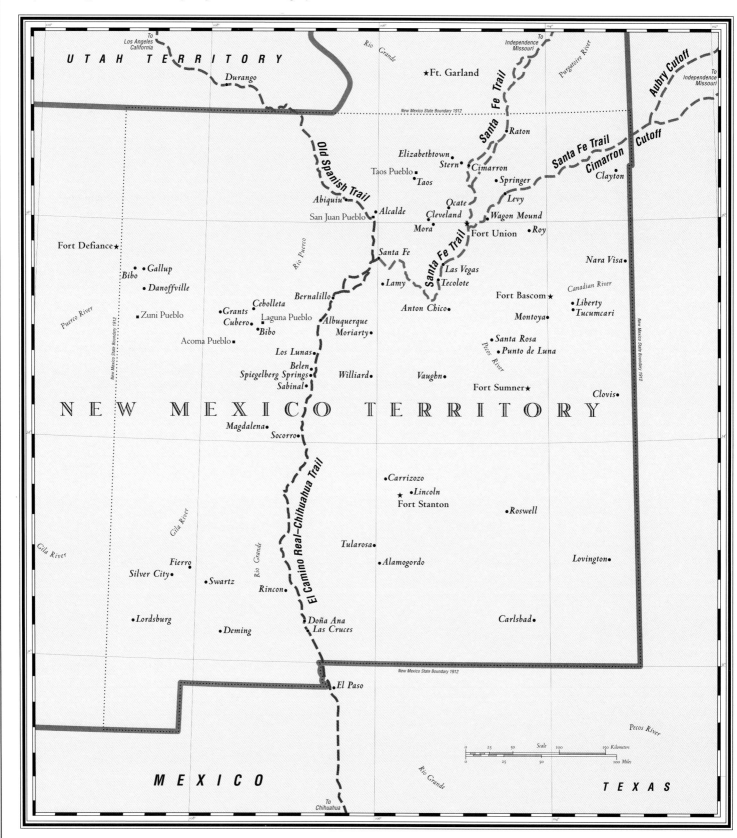

UTAH TERRITORY

To
Los Angeles
California

Durango

Rio Grande

To
Independence
Missouri

Purgatoire River

★ Ft. Garland

New Mexico State Boundary 1912

Santa Fe Trail

Aubry Cutoff

To
Independence
Missouri

Raton

Santa Fe Trail

Cimarron Cutoff

Old Spanish Trail

Elizabethtown

Stern

Cimarron

Clayton

Taos Pueblo

Taos

Springer

Abiquiu

Ocate

Levy

San Juan Pueblo

Alcalde

Cleveland

Wagon Mound

Mora

Roy

Fort Union

Fort Defiance ★

Santa Fe

Nara Visa •

Rio Puerco

Bibo

Gallup

Las Vegas

Santa Fe Trail

Lamy

Tecolote

Fort Bascom ★

Canadian River

Danoffville

Bernalillo

Anton Chico •

Liberty
Tucumcari

Puerco River

New Mexico State Boundary 1912

Zuni Pueblo

Cebolleta

Grants

Cubero

Laguna Pueblo

Montoya •

Albuquerque

Bibo

Moriarty

Santa Rosa

Pecos River

Punto de Luna

Acoma Pueblo ■

Los Lunas

Belen

Williard

Vaughn •

New Mexico State Boundary 1912

Spiegelberg Springs

Sabinal

Fort Sumner ★

Clovis •

N E W   M E X I C O   T E R R I T O R Y

Magdalena •

Socorro •

Carrizozo

El Camino Real–Chihuahua Trail

Lincoln

Fort Stanton

Roswell

Gila River

Tularosa

Rio Grande

Alamogordo

Lovington •

Gila River

Fierro

Silver City •

Swartz

Rincon •

Lordsburg

Deming

Doña Ana
Las Cruces

Carlsbad •

New Mexico State Boundary 1912

El Paso

Pecos River

Scale

M E X I C O

Rio Grande

T E X A S

To
Chihuahua

14

Alamogordo	Wolinger	Sabinal	
Alcalde	Ilfeld, Louis	(Socorro)	Appel, Nathan
Anton Chico	Dittenhoffer, Sam		Lesinsky, Henry
Belén	Freudenthal, Julius	San Juan	Eldodt, Nathan/Samuel
Bernalillo	Bibo, Nathan	Santa Rosa	Moise, Julius/Sigmund
	Seligman, Bernard	Silver City	Abraham
Carlsbad	Weiller, Marcel		Cohen
	Wertheim (Emma Vorenberg)		Lesinsky
Carrizozo	Ziegler, Albert		Schultz
Cebolleta	Bibo, Samuel/Simon		Weisl
Cimarron	Floersheim	Socorro	Appel, Nathan
Clayton	Ballon, Henry		Felsenthal, Louis
	Herzstein, Morris/Simon		Price, Marcus
	Weil, Max	Springer	Floersheim
Cleveland	Sachs, Moses	Taos	Beuthner,Solomon/Sampson/
	Vorenberg, Simon		Joseph
Clovis	Mandell		Gusdorf, Alexander
	Vohs, Samuel/Simon		Letcher, Adolph
Cubero	Barth, Solomon	Tecolote	Dittenhoffer, Sam
	Bibo, Samuel/Simon		Winternitz, David
Deming	Zeckendorf	Trinidad	
Doña Ana	Lesinsky	(Colorado)	Floersheim, Viola
Grants	Lesinsky		Ilfeld, Charles
	Lindauer, Sigmund	Tucumcari	Bonem, David/Joseph/Gilbert
Laguna	Bibo		Calisch, Albert
Las Cruces	Ashenfelter, S. M.		Goldenberg, Alex/Max
	Freudenthal		Kohn, Yetta
	Lesinsky, Solomon	Tularosa	Goldenberg
	Stern	Vaughn	Baer, Adolph
Liberty	Herzstein, Morris		Stern, Gus
Lincoln	Bernstein, Morris	Wagon Mound	Vorenberg, Simon/Walter/
	Lutz, Henry		Carrie
Los Lunas	Oppenheim, Max/Meno		
	Sachs, Moses		
Montoya		**Jewish Presence at Forts**	
(Tucumcari)	Calish, Albert/Belle	Fort Bascom	Gellerman, William
	Kohn, Howard/George/		Rosenwald, Emanuel
	Belle/Yetta	Fort Defiance	Spiegelberg, Lehman
	Waxman	Fort Garland	Meyer, Ferdinand
Mora	Biernbaum, Henry	Fort Stanton	Brunswick, Marcus
	Lowenstein, Rebecca	Fort Sumner	Holzman, Philip
	Strauss	Fort Union	Morrison, Arthur
	Vorenberg, Simon	Fort Wingate	Bibo, Nathan
Nara Vista			Spiegelberg, Solomon Jacob
(Clayton)	Lowenstein, Hugo		
Ocaté	Dittenhoffer, Sam	**German-Jewish Place Names**	
Puerto de Luna	Goldenberg	Bibo	
Raton	Floersheim	Danoffville	
	Ruben	Levy	
Roswell	Jaffa, Nathan	Spiegelberg Springs	
	Sulzbacher, Louis	Stern	
Roy	Floersheim	Sulzbacher	
		Swarts	

The Bibos

The ten Bibos who immigrated to New Mexico during the second half of the nineteenth century were children of a cantor in Bräkel, Westphalia. Nathan, Solomon, and Simon (following the footsteps of an uncle, Joseph Bibo, who also emigrated to New Mexico) launched their mercantile businesses after working briefly for the established firms of the Santa Fe Spiegelbergs and Albuquerque Zeckendorfs in the late 1860s. Contractors to the military posts of western New Mexico, the brothers established themselves in the general merchandise business in the vicinity of Laguna Pueblo. A fourth brother, Joseph, operated a similar business in Bernalillo, New Mexico. Simon and Solomon married local women: Simon wed Ramona Candelaria, and Solomon, Juana Valle, a native of Acoma Pueblo.

Trader Solomon Bibo, at Acoma Pueblo
Probably St. John's Day, 1883

Trader Solomon Bibo, husband of Juana Valle of Acoma Pueblo, with a group on top of the Governor's house, Acoma Pueblo. From left to right: San Juan Garcia, Solomon Bibo, Governor Anares Ortiz, and Martin Valle, Solomon's father-in-law.

Museum of New Mexico, Neg. No. 16460

While the Bibos were not influential in the economic or social development of New Mexico, their frontier affairs and genuine concerns for their Native American neighbors are familiar stories. Their lives are memorialized by two communities bearing their family name: one between Paguate and Seboyeta, New Mexico, and the other along old Route 66 in Arizona.

> The reason I left Germany for the United States ought to be mentioned here: to commemorate my ancestors who implanted the longing for this country in me and my folks.
>
> In the year of 1812, when Napoleon Bonaparte enlisted nearly all Europe then under his control, to furnish their contingent for him to invade Russia, a number of young fellows in Borgentreich, Westphalia, Prussia, were requested to enlist and amongst them was my grandfather, Lucas Rosenstein. . . .
>
> He preferred to go away, and not serve the French authorities, and he, with a number of young friends, all of whom had served the Prussian government, left for Holland and at Antwerp took passage in a sailing vessel, and after an eventful voyage of seventy-five days on the Atlantic arrived in Philadelphia in September, 1812. He returned to Prussia in 1820.

Whenever in vacation time I visited my grandparents, I loved to hear his stories of the early family life, and the equal rights and liberty of the people and their reverence for the father of our country, George Washington.

Whenever he spoke of him he uncovered his head, and also with grateful remembrance spoke of the kindness and hospitality of the Quakers and other early settlers in Pennsylvania.

I could not please the old man more than address him with 'Hello Grandpa,' or 'How do you do,' and greet him with English phrases which I had studied in school or from an English grammar which he had given me when I was about eight years old. In 1860 or 1859, one of his sons, Joseph Rosenstein, came to New Mexico, was in business at Santa Fe, and he died in 1865 and is buried in the Odd Fellows' Cemetery at Santa Fe.

—Nathan Bibo,
Reminiscences of Early New Mexico

Herman Wertheim's Passport Photo (Detail)

Early twentieth century

Herman Wertheim was a successful merchant for several decades. He established a general store in the mid-1880s in an existing adobe building at the center of the village of Doña Ana in south-central New Mexico. It was called "Geronimo's" because Herman was referred to by many as "Geronimo Wertine," an Hispanicized version of his name. Adjacent to the store was another adobe structure in which Wertheim and his relatives lived.

The Wertheim site was excavated by the New Mexico State University archaeological field school in 1998.

Courtesy New Mexico Heritage Center, New Mexico State University

R. W. and M. H. Isaacs

1883–84

Robert Wolf Isaacs was born in Victoria, Australia, and came to the United States from London with his parents in 1871. His family settled in Cincinnati and from there moved first to Trinidad, Colorado, and eventually to Clayton, New Mexico. "Bob" Isaacs tried gold mining and worked as a peddler before moving to Clayton.

Isaacs Family Collection

The Freudenthals

Las Cruces, 1864

Several Jewish pioneers settled in southern New Mexico, worked together, and were related, such as the Lesinsky-Freudenthal-Solomon clan. This view of Las Cruces, with the imposing St. Geneviève Catholic Church, would have been a familiar scene to all who lived there. The original St. Geneviève's was built of adobe in 1859 and by 1887 was replaced by this much larger church, which was torn down in 1968. A bank now occupies the site.

Courtesy Rio Grande Historical Collections, New Mexico State University Library

Phoebus Freudenthal

c. 1895

Born in Germany, Phoebus arrived in Las Cruces in the late 1860s, at age thirteen. He immediately went to work for his cousin Henry Lesinsky, and then worked for his brother-in-law at the Longfellow Copper Mining Company in Arizona for twelve years.

Courtesy Rio Grande Historical Collections, New Mexico State University

Anna Freudenthal Solomon and Isidor Solomon

c. 1890

Anna was the sister of Phoebus Freudenthal and the wife of Isidor Solomon. Arriving in Las Cruces with her husband, Anna notes in her memoirs that her parents and her husband's parents "were old friends."

The Solomon family moved from Las Cruces and opened a store and hotel in Solomonville, Arizona, in 1876. Eventually they also became involved in banking.

The Grants

Following his elder brother to New Mexico, Henry Grant arrived from Poland in the mid-1870s, went first to Missouri, and finally settled in Abiquiú, then a remote village in northwest New Mexico. He ran a general merchandise store on the plaza. Henry and his wife, Sarah, had four children: David, Hilda, Frances, and Joseph.

Henry Grant's Children

c. 1902

This photograph was taken near the Abiquiú village plaza. Shown here are Joseph, the youngest; Frances, who became a journalist and traveled throughout the world; and David. Hilda, the elder daughter, is not pictured.

Courtesy David Grant, Albuquerque

The Henry Grant Family

1910

Courtesy David Grant, Albuquerque

The Gusdorfs

The Gusdorf brothers, Alexander and Gerson, nephews of Zadoc and Abraham Staab, came to New Mexico from their home in Pyrmont, Westphalia, Germany. Upon his arrival in 1864, Alexander worked for a time in his Uncle Zadoc Staab's mercantile business and then opened his own stores in Taos and Elizabethtown. Gerson arrived in 1883 and worked first for his brother, and then at their uncle's store, Z. Staab & Bro. Later Gerson developed interests in mining and the sheep business, then bought his brother's mercantile concern around 1905.

Gerson married the daughter of an early Santa Fe pioneer, Simon Wedeles. Alexander returned to Germany in 1878 to marry Bertha Ferse of Oberlistingen (near Kassel, in the Duchy of Hesse-Kassel, in central Germany).

It is erroneously said that Alexander built the first steam flour mill in New Mexico (which burned in 1895). Actually, the first steam-powered grist-mill, which was operating by 1858, was built by Joseph Hersch of Santa Fe..

Alexander and Bertha, who lived in their large home near Taos Plaza, entered into the hotel business and began patronizing the local artist colony by allowing works to be hung in the lobby of what became the famous Don Fernando Hotel. Unfortunately their building burned to the ground in 1933, destroying an unknown number of works by the Taos Society of Artists.

Gerson Gusdorf As a Young Man

1894

Brother of Alexander, Gerson started his career as a salesman for Z. Staab & Bro. of Santa Fe. In 1907 Gerson opened his store on the Taos Plaza, which is said to have had the largest stock of general merchandise in the region.

E. Gusdorf Collection (G14/31A)

Alexander Gusdorf General Merchandise Store, Taos

1902

Alexander Gusdorf arrived in Taos in 1864, at age fifteen, to work for Z. Staab & Bro. Five years later he began his own business in Peñasco, New Mexico. He moved to Taos in 1880, built a steam-powered flour mill, and operated his store on the west side of the Taos Plaza until 1904.

Courtesy Kit Carson Historical Museum, Weimer Collection, Taos

The Manasses

Samuel, Solomon, and, eventually, Gustave Manasse, of Aachen, Rhineland, Germany, had all settled in Las Cruces by the 1890s. After Solomon died in 1906, Sam and Gus carried on the thriving family business, Manasse Brothers Dry Goods Store, and also were engaged in mining and real estate in the region. In 1917 Sam and Gus served as organizing directors of the Farmers' Trust and Savings Bank in Las Cruces, which later merged with the First National Bank there. Gus acted as mayor of Las Cruces from 1934 to 1936.

Manasseh Ben Israel
1636

Etching by Rembrandt.
Courtesy Rijksmuseum Amsterdam

The Manasse Brothers
c. 1880

left to right: Samuel, Solomon, and Gus Manasse
Courtesy Mr. I. T. "Mickey" Schwartz, Las Cruces

Tobacco Flask
1901

Possibly used as a container for *punché*, a locally grown tobacco, this rawhide flask bears the name of its owner, H. C. Ilfeld. Herman Ilfeld was the first of the Ilfeld brothers to arrive in New Mexico. He became a partner in the mercantile firm of Elsberg and Amberg in the 1860s. He married Henrietta Spiegelberg.

Palace of the Governors Collections

Table Linen
1865

According to a note left by Mrs. Noa (Helen) Ilfeld, "These pieces of stamped linen originally came from Germany in the year 1865. Embroidery done in later years." Most items brought from Germany by Jewish immigrants were not so well documented.

Palace of the Governors Collections (1075/45AB)

Cigarette Paper Bag
1870–1872

Described by Willi Spiegelberg as "Handmade bead cigarette paper bag used by the New Mexican for placing therein dried corn leaves, 'hojas,' which they used instead of cigarette paper." (Signed Willi Spiegelberg)

On loan from Felix and Susan (Spiegelberg) Warburg,
San Francisco, California

Chapter Two *Economic Activities & Politics*

Albuquerque Street Scene
1882 (see page 34)

A chance to improve one's economic life made New Mexico attractive to many. Here was a place that in 1846 had just become a U.S. territory. Here was a ground-floor opportunity for ambitious, energetic young businessmen to better their fortunes in a variety of ways. Mining ventures, land speculation, and the shipping of agricultural goods stimulated the skills and imaginations of entrepreneurs. The railroad, a means of cheap and rapid transportation, offered another kind of opportunity, one that redefined business. With its arrival in 1879, businesses grew from storefronts to mercantile houses that either expanded into railroading, livestock, land investment, and banking or split into specialized areas. General stores became obsolete as retailers specialized in hardware, clothing, jewelry, liquor, wool, and hide businesses. Las Vegas merchant Charles Ilfeld founded his mercantile store with one motto, "Wholesalers of Everything," and maintained warehouses for wool, piñon, hides, and goods throughout the state. Ilfeld, like many others, also functioned as financier of much of the commerce of Northern New Mexico.

While the Jewish merchants as a whole have been credited with introducing the capitalist system to a largely barter-driven society, they were equally adept in using existing and regressive economic systems to their advantage. Among mining and ranching towns, merchants established near–company stores in which their employees could redeem their weekly pay. The *partido* contract, not unlike the sharecropping system of the South, was widely used in agricultural partnerships by Hispano and mercantile capitalists. In such a contract, one party agreed to lend its sheep to another in exchange for payment from the proceeds of the wool. More often than not, the borrower carried the burden for a lost or sick sheep. Charles Ilfeld and Louis Freudenthal, among others, were very successful in combining traditional partido and capital systems to build flourishing mercantile businesses.

Charles Ilfeld engaged in several early learning experiences, with such associates as Adolph Letcher. Young Ilfeld clerked for Letcher in Taos for two years during the late 1860s. Foreseeing opportunities in the town of Las Vegas, the two loaded seventy-five burros with merchandise and moved there to form the partnership of A. Letcher and Company.

In other regions of New Mexico as well, towns like Gallup became gateways for rail development into Arizona. Jewish pioneers ventured into lumbering and ranching, while also establishing business relations with the Navajo and Zuni Indians. The town of Seligman, Arizona, is a vestige of this western movement. Anna Solomon journeyed from Poland, where she helped run the family store, to Las Cruces, and on to what became Solomonville, Arizona. Eventually she took ownership of a well-known hotel, which sported the area's finest dining room. At its regular masquerade balls, she and her husband dressed as George and Martha Washington.

In time, the Jewish community became stronger, making its economic mark in the early 1900s. Outside of the major cities, for example, in southern New Mexico, its members pioneered in agriculture and international trade, while in the north R. W. Isaacs and Phil Denitz opened the first hardware store in Clayton in the late 1890s. Four years later Isaacs claimed sole ownership and moved the business to its current location on Main and 1st Streets in downtown Clayton. In 1905 he married Mary Alice Stubbs, the Protestant daughter of a local homesteader who converted to Judaism.

On the plaza of the capital city, Emil and Johanna Uhlfelder opened the White House, a dry goods store with ready-to-wear clothing, in 1912 and established their name and reputation beyond Santa Fe early on. Emil Uhlfelder, a native of Regensburg, Bavaria, had come to the West in 1879 to participate in the frontier merchandise business. After he died in 1916 at the age of fifty-five, his wife, Johanna, remarried, and her new husband, Morris Blatt, started a small but highly lucrative business empire. In 1924 Johanna Blatt's daughter, Pauline Uhlfelder, married Barnett W. Petchesky, owner of a local shoe store. Thus, the Guarantee Shoe Shop became part of the family business empire, for all intents and purposes. Although Morris Blatt died in 1944, and his wife sometime thereafter, the business continued, managed by the grandchildren in the same location on the Santa Fe Plaza. After the original White House business had been sold, Jean Petchesky and Marian Petchesky-Silver merged businesses to form the Guarantee Incorporated.

Another account finds Louis Gold (whose headstone reads *Luis*), an immigrant from Poland, merchandising in Santa Fe in the middle 1830s, at about the age of fifteen. If true, Louis would be the earliest documented Jew in New Mexico so far. Gold held grain contracts with the U. S. Army through the 1850s with his uncle, Joseph Hersch, "El Polaco." As his nickname indicates, Joseph Hersch emigrated to Santa Fe from Poland. Arriving prior to 1850, Hersch, too, was involved in merchandising. In about 1858, he also built the first steam-powered gristmill in the state using machinery purchased from a failed gold mine. The pair became land speculators in the Santa Fe region. Gold sons Abe and Jake pursued the retail curio trade in the capital city, and Abe also served as postmaster of Peñasco. Hersch and Gold were cantors for the first Yom Kippur observance, the Day of Atonement and holiest day of the year for the Jewish people, in 1860 at the Santa Fe home of the Spiegelbergs. Hersch and his wife, Rosalia, are buried in Santa Fe's pioneer non-Catholic Fairview Cemetery.

It appears that most Jewish settlers in New Mexico became merchants and proprietors of mercantile stores, and it is equally apparent that they frequently went into business with family members or sold mercantile businesses among themselves. The well-known example is the Bibo family. The children of a cantor in Bräkel, Westphalia, Germany, ten members of this family emigrated to New Mexico during the second half of the nineteenth century. Nathan, Solomon, and Simon Bibo launched their mercantile businesses after working briefly for the firms established by the Spiegelbergs in Santa Fe and the Zeckendorfs in Albuquerque in the late 1860s. As contractors to western New Mexico military posts, the brothers entered the general merchandise business near Laguna Pueblo. Simon wed Ramona Candelaria, a local woman, and Solomon married Juana Valle, an Acoma Pueblo native. The Bibos' frontier affairs and true concern for their Native American and Hispanic neighbors and families are familiar stories.

In 1850 approximately twenty identifiable Jewish pioneers lived in New Mexico Territory. Taking few detours, many came to Santa Fe with either the army or wagon trains, and some were peddlers before settling in towns. One of the earliest known Jews was merchant Solomon Jacob Spiegelberg, who along with his five brothers worked in the Spiegelberg store on the south side of the Santa Fe Plaza. While the store certainly was not an unprofitable enterprise, much of the Spiegelbergs' fortunes came through government contracts from Washington, D.C., to ship goods to and from the Indian reservations in New Mexico. As early as 1847, Nathan Appel, like many others, worked as a mercantile peddler throughout the region before settling in Socorro.

Many of these early German Jewish merchants, like the Spiegelbergs, Staabs, Jaffas, and some of the Ilfeld brothers, were successful. In addition, Charles Ilfeld and Max Nordhaus were very prosperous German-Jewish merchants in the territory and earned the respect of many of their customers and friends. Ilfeld commanded loyal responses from the likes of Stephen Elkins, Senator from West Virginia and former New Mexico congressional delegate, in addition to having friends like Montgomery Bell, a trusted agent who was most likely an ex-slave.

Despite overall successes, businesses were at the mercy of economic cycles. Due to declining business in Las Vegas and Santa Fe, the Ilfeld Company moved to Albuquerque. Elizabeth Nordhaus recalled that "[I]n 1911 my father [Max Nordhaus] who had been general manager of the Charles Ilfeld Co. since the age of twenty-one, moved to Albuquerque and established headquarters. . . . In the early twentieth century, there were five wholesale houses dealing in groceries, hardware and dry goods, plus numerous retail outlets in smaller communities, several sheep ranches, and for a short time, liquor wholesalers." Albuquerque merchants, and merchants like Nordhaus and Ilfeld who had moved to the city, enjoyed prosperity as the "New Town" created by the railroad grew and eventually merged with the original "Old Town" around the Plaza. The railroad transformed Albuquerque: a rural community of *ranchitos* and small farms quickly developed into the commercial and population hub of New Mexico.

Another mercantile businessman was Benjamin Loewenstein, who was born in Westphalia in 1828 and emigrated to the United States around 1844. After marrying Rachel Birnbaum in Philadelphia, he moved to New Mexico, settling in Mora possibly as early as 1866. By the early 1870s Loewenstein owned a trading post with Henry Birnbaum, of Trinidad, Colorado, who may have been Rachel's brother. After Phillip Strauss bought out Birnbaum, he and Loewenstein sold the business to Joe Harberg and his wife, Teckla (Back). The Harbergs in turn sold to Teckla's brothers, Morris and Sam Back, who maintained the store starting in 1895. In 1913 the Back brothers sold the business to their two brothers-in-law, Philip Steinfeld and Morris Waxman. Waxman was reportedly a cousin of Morris Back's son, Seymour. Meanwhile, Joe Harberg's brother, Carl, opened a store in Cleveland, just a few miles from Mora, with his partner, Simon Vorenberg. Vorenberg proceeded to establish the town's first post office, then moved his family to Wagon Mound, where he opened a new store that was more lucrative and longer-lived.

The period from 1860 to 1880 is considered the Golden Age for Jewish merchants in the West, a time of prosperity, success, and recognition. Jewish merchants became well known among the Territory's leaders. Some branched out from family enterprises to form partnerships with non-Jewish merchants. However, by 1900 New Mexico began to lose its attraction as an alluring frontier for adventurous Jewish youth. Peddlers and traders fell in importance as more and more specialized stores opened and additional competition arrived with the railroad. Las Vegas experienced a decline that had begun with the closing of Fort Union in 1891. An economic depression in 1893 and the continued expansion of the rail lines sent traffic to other areas. Albuquerque became the commercial center of the Territory, and then the Territory of New Mexico itself changed, becoming a state in 1912. Santa Fe began a transformation that would make it a national health and travel destination, which, in turn, stimulated new kinds of traders, those dealing in curios and Indian goods.

Merchants and entrepreneurs certainly had a major impact on the economic future of New Mexico. This impact was enhanced by the fact that many of the merchants were also founders or owners of banking institutions. Henry Tobias, author of *The History of the Jews in New Mexico*, states that:

> Although [the pioneers'] primary economic activity remained, for the most of them, their stores, the nature of their operations, as well as opportunity, led them into a diverse economic life. Most notable was the move into banking. Until 1870, no banks existed in New Mexico. The large merchants played the role informally. The safes of such persons as Abraham Staab became the "depository" of large sums of money belonging to the native representatives throughout New Mexico . . . . The Spiegelbergs even issued their own scrip as early as 1863, and outside of the use of gold and silver, their paper was probably more highly regarded than bank notes. . . . In 1890 Roswell acquired its own bank. Nathan Jaffa served as a vice-president and member of the board of directors . . . . In 1900 Jaffa associated himself with the new Citizens Bank, where he served as cashier and on the board of directors. The new bank specialized in ranch and livestock loans.

The Spiegelbergs' Second National Bank, charted in 1872 in Santa Fe, was the most ambitious venture in banking involving Jews, but not the only one. Toward the end of the 1870s, Joseph Rosenwald became one of the organizers and directors of the San Miguel National Bank in Las Vegas. However, even after banks appeared, mercantile houses long remained de facto bankers for many of their customers.

Evidently a great change took place in business capitalism in territorial New Mexico with the arrival of the railroad in the 1880s, and the German Jew was key to the encouragement and development of New Mexico's growth. As William Parish, biographer of the Ilfeld Company, explains:

> We are picturing, too, an economy with a strongly unfavorable balance of trade that resulted in money being scarce commodity—an economy that placed the merchants under great pressure to acquire monetary exchange. The most important single factor giving the initial momentum to sizable amounts of monetary exchange in New Mexico was the public works project of the day: the army forts . . . . When a close connection with an army fort existed, cash sales to military personnel were high. Adolph Letcher found this to be true in Taos, where his store was a convenient stopping place for traffic between Fort Marcy and Fort Garland. The cash could then be converted in Federal drafts on Eastern banks which were deposited with wholesaling houses in New York City. These eastern drafts could also be obtained, and in larger amounts, by filling supply contract for the forts and for the Superintendent of Indian Affairs. These contracts were particularly valuable to the merchant because they meant the purchase of local produce—corn, wheat, lumber, and meat—which permitted the merchant's customers to reduce their balance with him.

Despite the impact and significance German-Jewish mercantile and banking businesses may have had in the economic and—indirectly—social development of New Mexico, Jews could also be found in many other professions in the state while continuing to retain ties to mercantile businesses. As they diversified from retailing into wholesaling, banking, and real estate, many of New Mexico's Jewish pioneer families also participated in the one enterprise most characteristically associated with life in the West: ranching. Of these pioneer ranchers, several had had experience raising cattle in their German homeland, while others concentrated on sheep ranching to meet the Eastern markets' demand for wool. The Kohns in Montoya, the Herzsteins in Union County, Sol Floersheim east of Springer, the Ilfelds' Moon Ranch between Santa Rosa and Vaughn, the Moise brothers in Santa Rosa, and Sydney Gottlieb between Cubero and Grants all built significant ranching operations in the late nineteenth and early twentieth centuries. Several of them remain family ranches today. Some people, like Sigmund Nahm, participated indirectly in the ranching business. Nahm was a merchant in Las Vegas before he moved to other locales, and he and his partner, Isadore Stern, opened their Las Vegas business after the railroad arrived. Not surprisingly, particularly during the Civil War, Jews participated actively in the military. In 1862 a Confederate army recruited in Texas invaded New Mexico through El Paso. Two Civil War battles were fought in New Mexico, and ultimately the Union held fast and ended the Confederate intention to expand to the Pacific. Jewish pioneers served in the Union Army as soldiers and fought in both battles. Three Jewish soldiers died at the Battle of Valverde:

Private Emile Kahn, Corporal Jacob Levy, and Corporal Simon Rothschild. Rothschild and Levy are buried in Santa Fe's National Cemetery. Additionally, Solomon Spiegelberg (cousin to the Spiegelberg brothers) received a commission of captain, and Bernard Seligman also became a captain serving as quartermaster.

Other Jewish pioneers who joined the Union Army include Joseph Beuthner, captain, and his brother, Solomon, colonel. William Zeckendorf and Marcus Brunswick also attained officer ranks. New Mexico's best-known Jewish Union soldier was Louis Felsenthal, who recruited a company of volunteers, was elected captain, and led his men into battle at Valverde. He also saw duty protecting caravans on the Santa Fe Trail. Jews, such as Henry Lesinsky of Las Cruces, who did not participate in Civil War conflicts in New Mexico as soldiers supported the effort as sutlers or suppliers for the Union. The Spiegelberg brothers also served as sutlers to the New Mexico Volunteers from July 1861 until July 1864. Solomon Jacob Spiegelberg had begun this tradition, first by becoming a provisioner during the Chihuahua campaign in the Mexican War (1846–48) and later as sutler to Fort Marcy in Santa Fe.

Another occupation that attracted Jewish pioneers was mining, concentrated in southwestern New Mexico. Few, if any, actually worked in the mines, but some owned mines or pursued the mining industry. In this part of the state, Jewish entrepreneurs, lured at first by valuable minerals such as silver and copper, moved in as the area opened up to settlement. Families like the Abrahams, Schutzes, and Lindauers settled in the Silver City area. The Lesinskys and Freudenthals established themselves in Las Cruces but operated mines for copper, silver, and other valuable ores all over the southern part of the territory and into Arizona. As with the Abrahams, Max Schutz and his brother entwined themselves not only in the mining business, but also within the political and social life of the community.

David Abraham arrived in southwestern New Mexico in the late 1860s and settled in Silver City in 1871 to become a pillar of the community. Having received the first patent to a mining claim ever issued in New Mexico, he died in Silver City in 1894. Abraham built several substantial business structures while he engaged in real estate and mining transactions, as well as the mercantile business.

Jewish families' active participation in economic life evolved inevitably into political service. The political situation in New Mexico during the early Territorial period still resembled the Spanish political system, which was, as one political scientist put it, "neither elaborate nor busy." The situation suited Jewish settlers well, since their activities were as much political as civic. These activities somewhat increased in the later part of the century, as the Anglo-American political traditions began to take hold in the state.

Especially after 1880 and the coming of the railroad, New Mexican society underwent a period of rapid change. By 1900 many Jews had assumed roles in local politics. Louis Freudenthal became well known in southern New Mexico politics, and Samuel Klein served as mayor of Las Cruces. Albuquerque's first two mayors were Jewish pioneers and prominent members of the Jewish community: Henry N. Jaffa (1885) and Mike Mandell (1890). Alex Goldenberg was the first county commissioner of Quay County.

Yet no officeholder was more unusual than trader Solomon Bibo. Bibo showed interest in Acoma Pueblo beyond its economic aspects. He learned the language, became a licensed trader to the pueblo, and eventually married a granddaughter of then–pueblo governor Martin Valle. Acoma acknowledged Bibo's concern for their well-being by appointing him governor in 1888, a post he held several times.

Another politically active pioneer was Columbus Moise, the descendent of an Alsatian family who was born in New Orleans in 1855. Shortly after he came to New Mexico, Moise married Sophie Dunlop, who was a daughter of the former Episcopalian bishop for the New Mexico dioceses, and they set up house in Las Vegas. In 1875 nineteen-year-old Moise was elected the town's city attorney. In 1880 he was appointed Chief Justice of the Territorial Supreme Court. The active politician chaired the San Miguel County Democratic Committee and, in 1892, was sent as a delegate to the Democratic National Convention. The multitalented Moise also wrote short stories and poems. They appeared under his pen name, "C. Esiom," in *Harper's Magazine* and *The Century Magazine*. He died at the age of forty. His grandsons, Irvin and Joseph, became prominent attorneys, and relatives Sigmund and Julius Moise each served as mayor of Santa Rosa.

In Columbus, New Mexico, Lithuanian immigrant and New Mexico businessman Louis Ravel was another Jewish immigrant who served as mayor. He and his brother even survived a raid on the town by Mexican General Pancho Villa's soldiers. Villa and his group crossed the border from Mexico into Columbus on March 9, 1916, and led a charge through the town that broke down the door of the Ravel brothers' store. Town businesses were looted, buildings were burned, and some residents were killed. Further north, R. W. Isaacs, owner of a hardware store in Clayton, was a steadfast Democrat who served on the Clayton City Council and represented New Mexico's Democratic Party at three national conventions.

1800–1899 Arrivals

Adler, Aaron
Bloch (Block) brothers
Floersheim, Solomon
Goldenberg brothers (Alex, Hugo, Max)
Herzstein, Morris
Isaacs, Robert
Jacobs brothers (Ben, Sol)
Kempenich, Ludwig, *b. Neheim, Westphalia*
Kornberg, Louis
Lesser brothers (David, Louis)
Levinson, Seymour
Levy (Felipe, L. F.)
Lindauer, Sigmund, *b. Baden Province*
Lowitsky, Solomon
Manasse brothers (Samuel, Solomon, Gustave),
    b. Aächen, Germany
Mandell, Mike
Moise brothers (Julius, Sigmund), *b. Oberstein*
Nordhaus, Max, *b. Paderborn, Westphalia*
Oppenheim brothers
Praeger brothers
Ravel, Yerman, b. Lithuania
Rosenthal, N. L.
Salsbury, Samuel Gershon, *b. New York*
Sawyer, Z. B.
Schiff, Samuel
Seligman brothers (Julius, Siegfried, Ernest, Carl),
    b. Werden an der Ruhr
Solomon brothers (Isidor, Fred Z), *b. Posen, Prussia*
Spitz, Solomon, *b. Breslau, Silesia*
Weil, Max
Weinman brothers (David, Jacob)
Wertheim, Herman, *b. Helmarshausen, Hesse Kassel*

1900–1920 Arrivals

Blatt, Herman
Danoff, Samuel Jessel, *b. Gebernia, Vilna, Lithuania*
Fleisher, Alphonse
Jacobson, Jacob
Kahn, Benedict, *b. Goddelsheim, Waldeck, Germany*
Kahn, Gustave, *b. "Empire of Germany"* (on naturalization document)
Moreel, Sam, *b. Riga, Latvia*
Ravel brothers (Sam, Louis, Arthur),
    b. Saiki, Lithuania
Schweizer, Herman, *b. Eppingen, Germany*
Seligman, Morris, *b. Meretz, Lithuania*
Taichert brothers (Joseph, Milton, Daniel),
    b. Schelinin Memel River, Germany; Taurog and Sudarg, Lithuania
Uhlfelder, Emil

BANKING

The Spiegelbergs' Second National Bank, chartered in 1872 in Santa Fe, was the most ambitious Jewish venture into banking with the exception of Joseph Rosenwald's San Miguel National Bank, in Las Vesas, New Mexico. Until 1870, no banks existed in the Territory.

Stage Coming into Santa Fe
c. 1885

The Exchange Hotel (now La Fonda), San Francisco Street.
Museum of New Mexico, Neg. No. 10672

Lehman Spiegelberg
c. 1870

Courtesy Ken M. Deitch (great-grandson of Lehman Spiegelberg), Carlisle, Massachusetts

Stock Certificate

1876

Issued to Mrs. Flora Spiegelberg by the Second National Bank of New Mexico, this certificate for ten shares is signed by her husband, Willi Spiegelberg, as president of the bank.

On loan from Felix & Susan (Spiegelberg) Warburg, San Francisco, California

Spiegelberg Brothers' Shinplaster

n.d.

During the Civil War businesses issued scrip that was circulated among their respective customers and even honored by other business houses. Every note was worth fifty cents if presented in amounts totaling five dollars. The scrip, called shinplaster, was redeemed in U. S. currency when the war ended.

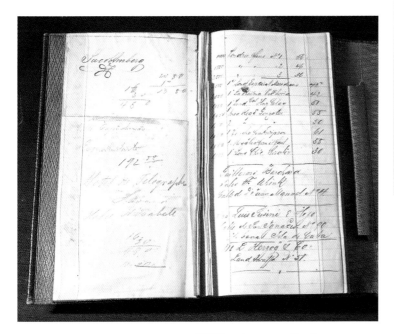

Wallet Account Book

c. 1860

Book belonged to Jacob Amberg

On loan from the Robert Amberg Family

Abe Spiegelberg

1919

Oil on canvas by B. J. O. Nordfeldt (1878–1955)

Born in 1848, Abe Spiegelberg was only ten years old when he came to Santa Fe with his father, Solomon. Abe was a merchant and trader all his life and over the years assembled one of the finest collections of Indian blankets in the Southwest. He was second cousin to the first Spiegelbergs to immigrate into New Mexico, brothers Solomon Jacob, Willi, Lehman, Levi, and Emanuel.

Gift of Mrs. B. J. O. Nordfeldt, Museum of Fine Arts Collections, Museum of New Mexico

Charles Ilfeld, Merchant and Financier

Charles Ilfeld Company

c. 1920

Charles Ilfeld Company, at Copper and North 1st Street, Albuquerque.

Courtesy Albuquerque Museum, Ward Hicks Collection, Neg. No. 1982.180.682

Charles Ilfeld

n.d.

Museum of New Mexico
Neg. No. 26139

Charles Ilfeld and Max Nordhaus were the most successful German Jewish merchants in the territory, but it is not likely they were atypical to accept abilities wherever and in whatever bodily case they could be found. . . . The result was to encourage social and economic associations that were productive to people in all walks of life. . . . The same could be said of the Spiegelbergs, Staabs, Jaffas and other Ilfeld brothers. . . . Ilfeld could command the same loyal response from Stephen Elkins, Senator from West Virginia and former delegate from New Mexico to Congress, as he did from his trusted agent and friend, Montgomery Bell—most probably an ex-slave. . . .

—William J. Parish
The German Jew and the Commercial Revolution in Territorial New Mexico, 1850–1900

The North Side of the Las Vegas Plaza

c. 1887

Museum of New Mexico, Neg. No. 14719

In 1911 my father [Max Nordhaus, Charles Ilfeld's brother-in-law] *who had been general manager of the Charles Ilfeld Co. since the age of twenty-one, moved to Albuquerque and established headquarters. . . . By 1911 there were five wholesale houses dealing in groceries, hardware and dry goods, plus numerous retail outlets in smaller communities, several sheep ranches, and for a short time, liquor wholesalers.*

—Elizabeth Nordhaus Minces,
The Family: Early Days in New Mexico

Elsberg & Amberg

After a time of prospecting silver claims in Piños Altos, Jacob Amberg joined forces in 1855 with Gustave Elsberg, one of the first Jewish merchants in Westport, Kansas. A year later, Elsberg & Amberg moved to Santa Fe. The firm financed Adolph Letcher in his Taos business venture, A. Letcher & Co., where eighteen-year-old Charles Ilfeld first worked as a clerk. Eventually Ilfeld became a partner, bought out Letcher, and created Charles Ilfeld Company in Las Vegas. The Ilfelds were cousins of Elsberg and Amberg.

The Elsberg & Amberg Wagon Train in Santa Fe's Plaza
October 1861
Museum of New Mexico, Neg. No. 11254

Rosenwald Hall

c. 1882–85

Rosenwald Hall on Railroad Avenue, Las Vegas, New Mexico

Museum of New Mexico, Neg. No. 0434

Provisions Hamper

c. 1870

This wicker hamper was used by Jewish merchant Emanuel Rosenwald of Las Vegas when he traveled the Santa Fe Trail to Missouri to purchase trade goods. Arriving in Las Vegas in the 1860s, Emanuel and his brother, Joseph, were merchants, freighters, sutlers, Indian traders, government contractors, and bankers.

Palace of the Governors Collections

Albuquerque's "New Town" booms

Albuquerque merchants enjoyed prosperity as the "New Town" created by the railroad grew and eventually merged with the original "Old Town" around the Plaza. The railroad transformed Albuquerque from a rural community of *ranchitos* and small farms into the commercial and population center of New Mexico.

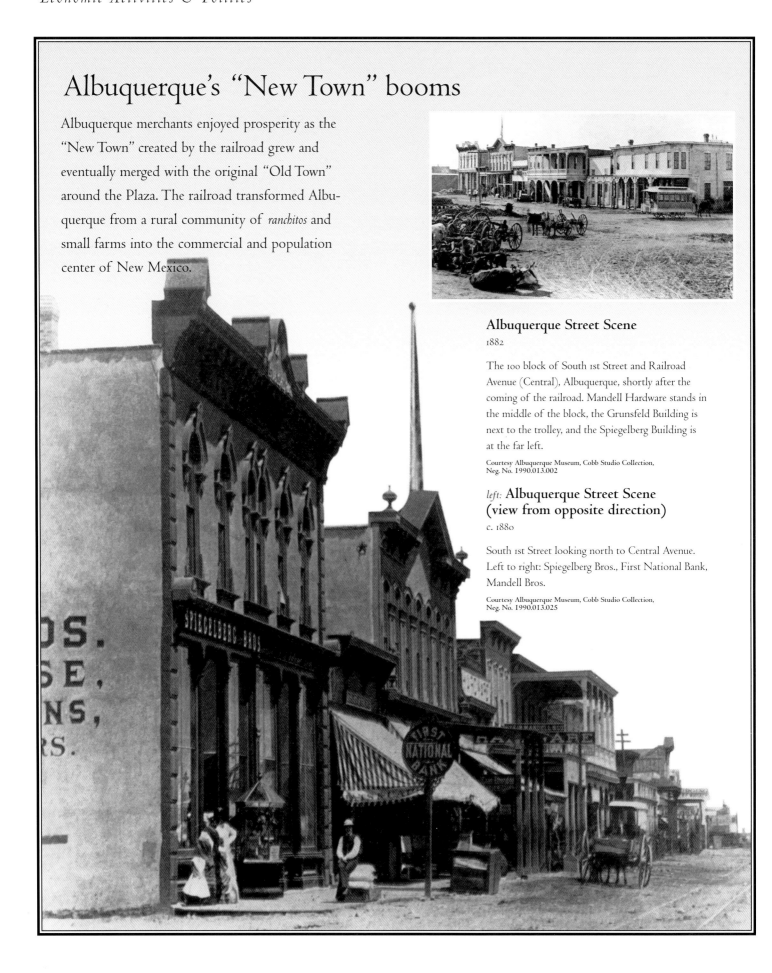

Albuquerque Street Scene
1882

The 100 block of South 1st Street and Railroad Avenue (Central), Albuquerque, shortly after the coming of the railroad. Mandell Hardware stands in the middle of the block, the Grunsfeld Building is next to the trolley, and the Spiegelberg Building is at the far left.

Courtesy Albuquerque Museum, Cobb Studio Collection, Neg. No. 1990.013.002

left: **Albuquerque Street Scene (view from opposite direction)**
c. 1880

South 1st Street looking north to Central Avenue. Left to right: Spiegelberg Bros., First National Bank, Mandell Bros.

Courtesy Albuquerque Museum, Cobb Studio Collection, Neg. No. 1990.013.025

Mayor Henry Jaffa and His Wife

1895

Albuquerque's first mayor, Henry Jaffa, and his wife, Bessie, at the opening of the Commercial Club

Courtesy Center for Southwestern Research, University of New Mexico, Cobb Collection, Neg. No. 000-119-0762

Grunsfeld Building

c. 1900

Grunsfeld Building, at the corner of 2nd and Gold Streets, Albuquerque.

Courtesy Albuquerque Museum, Cobb Studio Collection, Neg. No. 1990.013.014

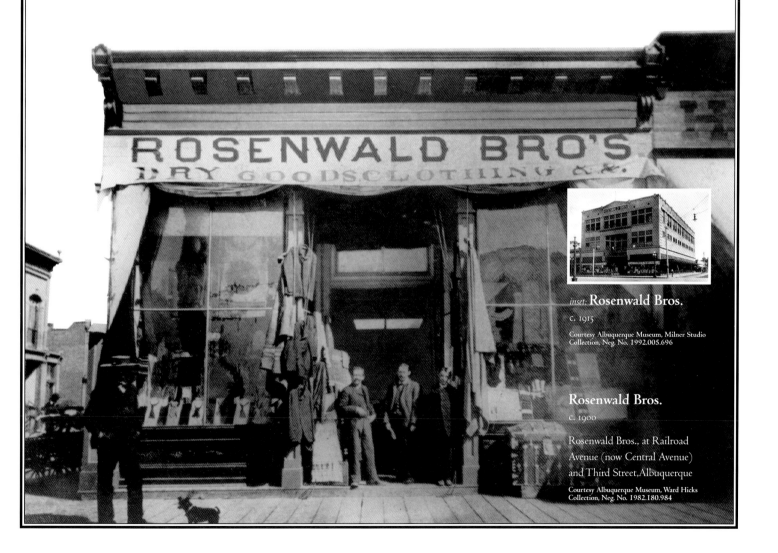

inset: **Rosenwald Bros.**

c. 1915

Courtesy Albuquerque Museum, Milner Studio Collection, Neg. No. 1992.005.696

Rosenwald Bros.

c. 1900

Rosenwald Bros., at Railroad Avenue (now Central Avenue) and Third Street, Albuquerque

Courtesy Albuquerque Museum, Ward Hicks Collection, Neg. No. 1982.180.984

The "Bernalillo Merc"

The Seligman brothers arrived in San Francisco from Werden-ahm-Rhur when Siegfried was twenty and Julius only sixteen. Around 1898 they bought the Bernalillo store owned by their cousins, the Bibos, and renamed it the Bernalillo Mercantile Company. For decades, "Bernalillo Merc" was an integral part of the community and served as a key training post for many young German immigrants as well.

[In 1910] my father borrowed the 300 marks for my steamship passage from Carlshafen. . . . My first job in this country was in Bernalillo, New Mexico, and I got a salary of $20 a month and room and board. . . . The entire personnel of the Bernalillo Mercantile Company was then composed of boys who had come over to the United States from Germany. . . . The German Jewish boys did not stay for very long with the Bernalillo Mercantile Company. After a short time, they would leave the employ of the store and would open up their own stores in the various towns of New Mexico. This is how the German Jewish boys got their start in business.

— Herman Wertheim,
Memoirs of Herman Wertheim

My father [Sig Nahm] had by then gone into business for himself. He had come to New Mexico, all the way from the Rheinpfalz, as a boy of sixteen. . . . In those days, young immigrant boys intent on a mercantile career learned their trade the direct way. They undertook what was really an apprenticeship either with Loewenstein, Strouse and Company in Mora or at the Bernalillo Mercantile Company some twenty miles from Albuquerque. They learned, if they didn't know already, not only how to be efficient and courteous clerks but also the intricacies of a trade which hadn't changed much from that practiced on the Santa Fe-St. Joseph, Missouri covered wagon route.

—Milton C. Nahm,
Las Vegas and Uncle Joe: The New Mexico I Remember

Bibo & Co. General Merchandise
May 3, 1903

standing: Joseph Bibo (in the bow tie), his wife on his left, and Ernest Seligman on her left.
seated: James Bibo (holding the dog), his brother, Milton, on his right, and his sister, Reina, in the wagon.
Courtesy Susan Kennedy, Albuquerque

Spitz Gift Box
n.d.

Spitz Jewelry and Gift Shop was a mainstay on the south side of the Santa Fe Plaza for many years.

Fray Angélico Chávez History Library, Palace of the Governors

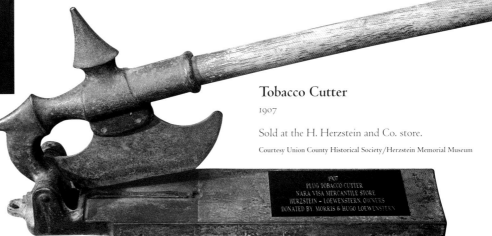

Tobacco Cutter
1907

Sold at the H. Herzstein and Co. store.

Courtesy Union County Historical Society/Herzstein Memorial Museum

Swastika Filigree Pin
Late nineteenth century

Solomon Spitz, born in Breslau, Germany, came to Santa Fe in 1880 and established himself as a jeweler. An 1886–1887 catalog of his "Mexican" filigree selection indicates intricate pieces, including those made to resemble the San Miguel Church in Santa Fe. There were also requests for swastika pins, an ancient symbol that long predated the Nazi movement in Germany.

Palace of the Governors Collections (9812/45)

Brush
c. 1900

Sold at Simon Herzstein's store and used by Mrs. Ana Anaya, a seamstress who worked for Simon for more than forty years. The inscription reads: "Herzstein's Clayton, New Mexico—Dalhart, Texas / If it's from Herzstein's it's correct." The Herzsteins' business eventually expanded throughout northeastern New Mexico and into the Texas panhandle.

Courtesy Union County Historical Society/Herzstein Memorial Museum

The Herzsteins

Morris Herzstein was a descendent of a Sephardic family that originated in Spain and had moved to the German town of Thulen, where he was born in 1869.

Morris followed his older brother, Nachman, to Pennsylvania in 1882 and in 1886 moved to New Mexico. For four years he sold goods from a pack he carried as he traveled through Colfax, Mora, and San Miguel counties.

In 1890 Morris opened his first store in Casa Blanca, Union County, New Mexico. Two years later he took his business to Liberty (Tucumcari), and in 1896 he moved to Clayton. There, he became prominent in business, community affairs, and politics, and served on the Clayton City Council as chairman of the County Democratic Central Committee.

It was in Clayton that Morris Herzstein joined with nephews Simon and Herbert and cousin Hugo Loewenstern to open one of the town's most notable mercantile firms, M. Herzstein and Company.

Nachman Herzstein, the first of the Herzsteins to emigrate from Thulen to the United States, stayed in Pennsylvania, where he had twelve children by two wives. At least six of his boys followed their Uncle Morris to New Mexico and worked with him at the family store.

Morris' younger brother, Levi, moved to Liberty in the early 1880s. In 1896 Levi was killed by the "Black Jack" Ketchum gang, after they robbed the family store.

Cream Separation Exhibition, Union County Fair, Clayton
September 1914

The Herzsteins worked with and were related to the Loewensterns. Other Jews, including R. W. Isaacs, also worked in Clayton. In 1898 he opened "Isaacs," the same Clayton store that his descendants still own and operate.

Museum of New Mexico, Neg. No. 14623

Herzstein Old Reliable Store, Clayton

June 13, 1908

Courtesy Union County Historical Society/Herzstein Memorial Museum

S. Herzstein Ready-to-Wear Store, Clayton

c. 1905

Reflecting the move from general merchandise to specialized stores, Morris' nephew, Simon, opened his own business. Nachman's son, Leonard, is standing next to the pole.

Courtesy Union County Historical Society/Herzstein Memorial Museum

The Golds

Louis Gold immigrated from Poland and was merchandising in Santa Fe by 1835, the earliest documented Jewish merchant immigrant in the Territory. With his uncle, Joseph Hersch, Gold held grain contracts with the U. S. Army through the 1850s and was involved in land speculation in the Santa Fe area. Son Abe Gold became postmaster of Peñasco, New Mexico.

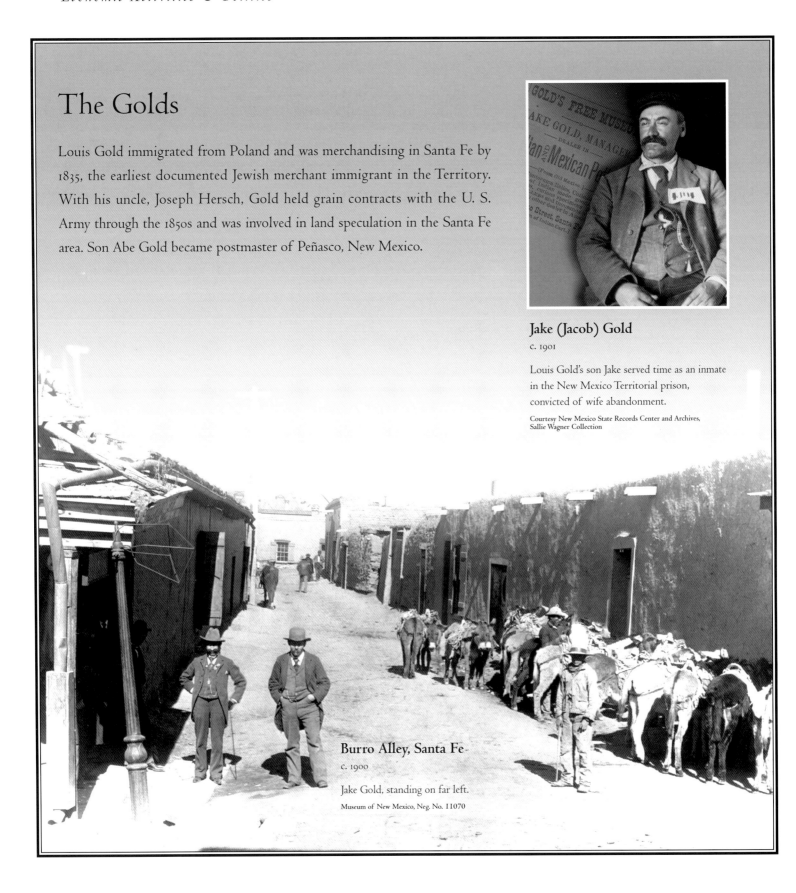

Jake (Jacob) Gold
c. 1901

Louis Gold's son Jake served time as an inmate in the New Mexico Territorial prison, convicted of wife abandonment.

Courtesy New Mexico State Records Center and Archives, Sallie Wagner Collection

Burro Alley, Santa Fe
c. 1900

Jake Gold, standing on far left.

Museum of New Mexico, Neg. No. 11070

I recall that in my younger days I used to sit in the curio shop of Jake Gold by the hour, trying to study and learn from him what constituted a good blanket.

—Arthur Seligman
Governor of New Mexico

above: **Gold's Old Curio Shop**
c. 1880

Interior of Jake Gold's shop.
Museum of New Mexico, Neg. No. 10729

right: **Gold's Old Curio Shop**
c. 1900

Jake Gold's curio shop on San Francisco Street, Santa Fe.
Museum of New Mexico, Neg. No. 10731

The Hersches

Joseph Hersch, aka "El Polaco," arrived in Santa Fe from Poland prior to 1850. An uncle of Louis Gold, Hersch also was in merchandising and during the 1850s developed lucrative contracts to supply corn and flour to the army.

Hersch also constructed the first steam-powered gristmill in New Mexico, about 1858, from machinery purchased from a failed gold mine.

Hersch and Gold were cantors for the first Yom Kippur observance at the home of the Spiegelbergs in Santa Fe.

Hersch's wife, Rosalia, brought her piano over the Santa Fe Trail. The couple are buried in Santa Fe's Fairview Cemetery.

Rosalia and Joseph Hersch
n.d.
Joseph Hersch established the first steam flour mill in New Mexico Territory.

Museum of New Mexico, Neg. Nos. 37783 & 37782

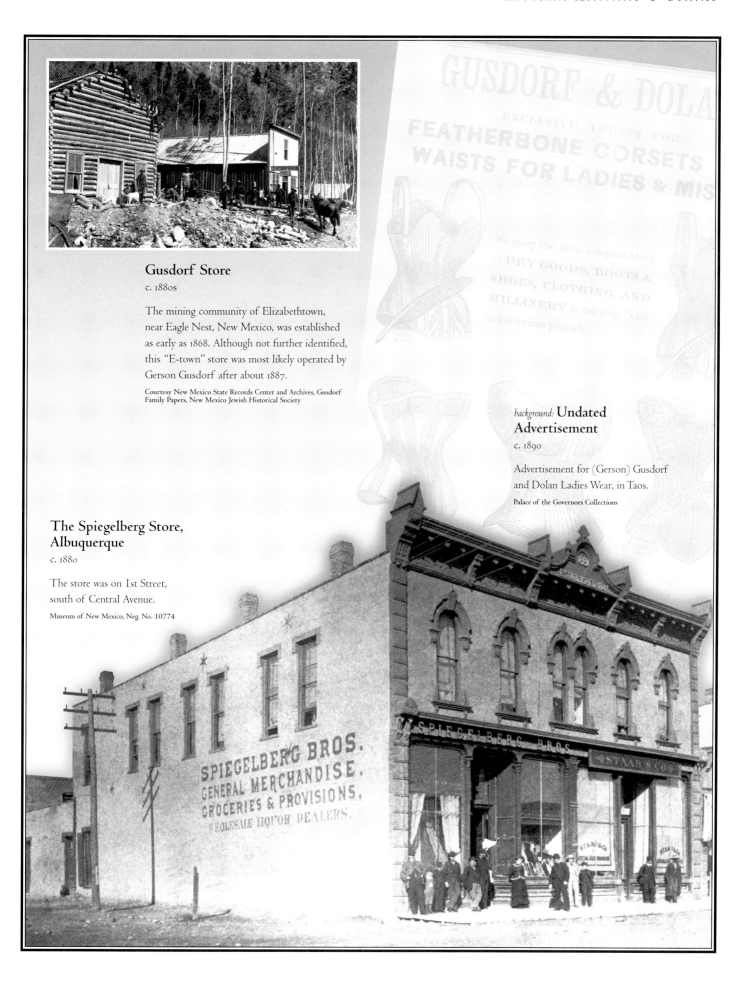

Gusdorf Store

c. 1880s

The mining community of Elizabethtown, near Eagle Nest, New Mexico, was established as early as 1868. Although not further identified, this "E-town" store was most likely operated by Gerson Gusdorf after about 1887.

Courtesy New Mexico State Records Center and Archives, Gusdorf Family Papers, New Mexico Jewish Historical Society

background: **Undated Advertisement**

c. 1890

Advertisement for (Gerson) Gusdorf and Dolan Ladies Wear, in Taos.

Palace of the Governors Collections

The Spiegelberg Store, Albuquerque

c. 1880

The store was on 1st Street, south of Central Avenue.

Museum of New Mexico, Neg. No. 10774

Taichert's Haberdashery

In 1898, at the age of 22, Joseph A. Taichert sailed alone from Hamburg, Germany to the United States. . . . In 1906, Joseph sent for his orphaned brothers. Nathan came to Louisville with Pinchas, 6, Daniel, 10, and Milton, age 13.

In 1905 Joseph travelled to Las Vegas, New Mexico, for the cure of asthma and tuberculosis. He learned to hunt and fish, opened Taichert's Haberdashery and bought hides, pelts, and wool from sheep growers.

In 1908, my father sent for Milton, ten years his junior, who joined the Joseph A. Taichert Company. . . .

My father and mother made preserves stored in a special room in the basement. He had a vegetable garden and a root cellar. We raised chickens and ducks until our neighbor Mrs. Arthur (Bessie) Ilfeld complained. He loved to fly fish in the Gallinas Canyon or at Peñasco and to go bird hunting with his English Springer Spaniel at Storrie Lake. Food, and its preparation, was always important to him. . . . Sometimes we went on picnics in the Gallinas Canyon, always with a 12-gauge shotgun, a shovel, and wooden plank in the back seat floor of the car. My mother hated these outings and would say, 'If the gun goes, I'm going to stay home.' She and the gun always went. My mother called Las Vegas the 'jumping-off' place, and I remember saying, 'Mamma—where do you jump?'

—Louise Taichert

Company Scale
Late nineteenth century

Scale used at Floersheim
Mercantile Company.

Courtesy Barry Floersheim, Roy

Office Interior
c. 1900

Floyd S. Ivey and Bob Aldridge
inside the office of the Floersheim
Mercantile Company.

Courtesy Bary Floersheim, Roy

left: **Milton Taichert**

1909

Milton Taichert at the entrance to
J. A. Taichert's store in Las Vegas.

Courtesy Louise C. Taichert, Mill Valley, California

below: **Retail License**

1917

Floersheim Mercantile Company.

Courtesy Bary Floersheim, Roy

47

Complex Connections in Mora

A complicated interweaving of family and business connections occurred in Mora, as elsewhere in New Mexico.

Benjamin Loewenstern, born in Westphalia in 1828, immigrated to the United States around 1844. He married Rachel Birnbaum in Philadelphia, then moved to New Mexico, settling in Mora, possibly as early as 1866. By the early 1870s Loewenstern owned a "trading post" with Trinidad resident Henry Birnbaum, who may have been Rachel's brother.

Phillip Strauss bought out Birnbaum, then he and Loewenstern sold the business to Joe Harberg and his wife, Teckla (Back) Harberg. The Harbergs sold to Teckla's brothers, Morris and Sam Back, who kept the store from 1895 to 1913. (Teckla, Morris, and Sam's mother was Amalia Strauss.)

The Back brothers sold the store to their two brothers-in-law, Philip Steinfeld and Morris Waxman. Waxman was said to be a cousin to Morris Back's son, Seymour.

Meanwhile, Joe Harberg's brother, Carl, formed a partnership with Simon Vorenberg to open a store in Cleveland, just a few miles from Mora. Vorenberg established the first post office in Cleveland before moving his family to Wagon Mound, where he opened a more successful and longer-lived store.

**Carl Harberg (seated)
with Jicarilla Apaches**
n.d.

Rio Grande Historical Collections,
New Mexico State University Library

Vorenberg Store, Wagon Mound
c. 1916

Two cars in this photograph are camouflaged as duck blinds.

Courtesy Tresa Vorenberg, Santa Fe

The Isaacs

In 1898 R. W. Isaacs and Phil Denitz opened the first hardware store in Clayton. Four years later Isaacs took sole ownership of the business and moved it to its current location, on Main and First streets in downtown Clayton.

In 1905 Isaacs married Mary Alice Stubbs, the Protestant daughter of a homesteader in the area. She converted to her husband's religion. Isaacs was a staunch Democrat, who served on the Clayton City Council and represented New Mexico's Democratic Party at three national conventions.

inset, top right: **Isaacs Mercantile, Clayton**
c. 1908

background: **Isaacs Hardware Store, Clayton**
c. 1915

inset, lower right: **Alice Isaacs**
1905

foreground: **R. W. Isaacs**
n.d.

Courtesy R. W. Isaacs Family, Clayton

Views of the Isaacs'
Store Interior
n.d.
Courtesy R. W. Isaacs Family, Clayton

Right: Dr. W. Isaacs' Account
Statement for John Spring
1905

Courtesy R. W. Isaacs Family, Clayton

HOWARD KOHN

The White House

After working as a collector for Charles Ilfeld, 'Uncle' Sol Floersheim operated a small general store at Ocaté. In 1897, he opened a store in Springer, the trading point and nearest rail head for the vast area, with wagon trains hauling ranch supplies and provisions in eastern New Mexico and West Texas. . . .

He opened a branch store in Roy in 1902 to serve the El Paso & Southwestern rail line from Tucumcari to the Dawson coal fields. In 1916, a fire destroyed the Roy store, but a fireproof building was rebuilt shortly. . . .

When settlers came to file on 160-acre homesteads and soon became short on money, their credit was good until harvest at Floersheim's.

— Karl Guthman, former publisher, Roy

The White House
c. 1912

The White House, a dry goods and ready-to-wear store, was located on the east side of the Santa Fe Plaza.

Museum of New Mexico, Neg. No. 67593

Owners of the White House, in Santa Fe
c. 1917

Johanna (second from left) and her second husband, Morris Blatt (second from right), and their staff of the White House department store, later known as The Guarantee, on the Santa Fe Plaza.

Courtesy Carl Floersheim Jr., Albuquerque

Emil and Johanna Uhlfelder
Early 1900s

The Uhlfelders opened The White House department store on the Santa Fe Plaza in 1912. Emil served as secretary of Congregation Albert in Albuquerque from 1909 to 1912. After he died in 1916, Johanna carried on the family store. She later married Morris Blatt.

Courtesy Carl Floersheim Jr., Albuquerque

The Ranching Kohns

Howard Kohn
n.d.
Rancher and expert horseman.

Courtesy Yetta Kohn Bidegain and Phillip B. Bidegain, Tucumcari

Saddle and Bridle
n.d.

These belonged to Howard Kohn. The bit's shanks are engraved with his initials.

On loan from Yetta Kohn Bidegain and Phillip B. Bidegain, Tucumcari

Yetta Goldsmith was born in Bavaria in March 1843 and immigrated with her family to the United States when she was young. By 1857 she was living in Leavenworth, Kansas, and had married Samuel Kohn, from Pilsen.

After moving to Cherry Creek, Colorado, then returning to Leavenworth, Yetta and Samuel traveled the Santa Fe Trail to Las Vegas in the mid-1860s. On the way they saw buffalo and, in Las Vegas, were greeted by the sight of some men who had been hanged from the windmill tower in the town's plaza.

Undeterred, they stayed and opened Kohn's store, where they sold wood, hides, flour, and grain. The store was located on the same block with businesses owned by Marcus Brunswick and Charles Ilfeld.

Samuel died in 1878, leaving his widow with four children and the store. In true frontier fashion, Yetta Kohn continued to run the business. Four years later she moved her family to the village of La Cinta (near present-day Conchas Dam), where she opened a general store, became the village's postmistress, and ran a ferry across the Canadian River. With what little money she made, Yetta bought parcels of land and, in time, formed the 4V Ranch. At one point, she and her partners, who included son Howard, daughter Belle, Louis Sulzbacher, and Harry Waldo, owned 3,858 head of cattle.

Yetta and her family moved next to Montoya, where they purchased a store, opened a bank, and acquired land through the Homestead Act. They became influential enough to send another of her sons, Charles, to New Mexico's Constitutional Convention.

Her 4V Ranch became the basis of the T-4 Cattle Company, which remains in the family.

Samuel Kohn
c. 1870

Samuel Kohn, husband of Yetta Kohn, moved the family to Las Vegas, New Mexico.

Courtesy New Mexico State Records Center and Archives

Yetta Kohn
December 1896

Matriarch, rancher, businesswoman.

Courtesy Yetta Kohn Bidegain and Phillip B. Bidegain, Tucumcari

Sigmund Nahm was a merchant in Las Vegas before he moved to other locales. He and partner Isadore Stern opened their Las Vegas business after the railroad arrived.

My father's [Sig Nahm] venture had little to do with the Bell Ranch as such, although the old ledger of the business firm of Reuther and Nahm shows that various employees of that great company did trade with them. He and Fred Reuther, another somewhat older immigrant from Germany, set up in business at a hamlet called La Cinta, which I have never seen, but which, from all I can make out, fit into the pattern of such places in the Southwest on the edge of the Texas Plains. A crossroads and a bar and a store and a few houses made it up. But it was on the route of the Goodnight cattle trail, which was at the height of its traffic until the blizzard of 1885. Goodnight drove his great herds by way of eastern New Mexico to the pastures in Colorado and Wyoming and to the railheads in Kansas.

—Milton C. Nahm,
*Las Vegas and Uncle Joe:
The New Mexico I Remember*

Solomon Floersheim
n.d.

Solomon Floersheim was a pioneer merchant in Springer and Roy, and owner of the Jaritas Ranch, east of Springer.

Courtesy Carl Floersheim Jr., Albuquerque

I might mention that my father was five-feet tall and weighed 110-pounds, but he was packed full of dynamite, fearless and his hobby was licking men. He was unusually strong, very agile, a veritable tiger, and when he hit, a man went down.

—Carl Floersheim,
Memoir of Sol Floersheim

Sig Nahm, Las Vegas
n.d.

Museum of New Mexico, Neg. No. 154417

Soldiers and Sutlers

Jewish pioneers served the Union Army as soldiers and sutlers, the popular term for noncombantants who kept the soldiers provisioned.

Captain Louis Felsenthal
1866

Felsenthal, far left, with Army officers, Santa Fe

Museum of New Mexico, Neg. No. 56281

Captain Louis Felsenthal
1865

New Mexico's best-known Jewish Union soldier, Captain Louis Felsenthal, recruited a company of volunteers and subsequently was elected captain. He led his company into battle at Valverde and also saw duty protecting caravans on the Santa Fe Trail. Born in Iserlohn, Westphalia, Prussia, in 1832, Felsenthal arrived in New Mexico in 1858. The following year he became a founding member of the Historical Society of New Mexico.

Museum of New Mexico, Neg. No. 9872

The headstones in this photograph are reminders of the Jewish citizens who fought as United States Regular Army soldiers and were killed in 1862, fighting to preserve the Union.

Headstones
n.d.

226 Jacob Levy, and 227 Simon Rothschild,
National Cemetery, Santa Fe.

Mining

The lure of precious minerals attracted Jewish pioneers to southwestern New Mexico. Families such as the Abrahams, Schutzes, and Lindauers settled in the Silver City area, while the Lesinskys and Freudenthals went to the southern part of the territory and into Arizona in search of copper, silver, and other valuable ores.

Max Schutz
1882

In southwestern New Mexico, as the area opened up to settlement, Jewish entrepreneurs moved in, lured at first by valuable minerals, such as silver and copper.

As with the Abrahams of Silver City, Max Schutz and his brothers' lives entwined with the economic, political, and social life of the community. The photograph below shows the building occupied by the Schutz business from 1880 to 1883.

In the 1850s the first brick kilns were constructed. As a result, many buildings of that time were built with this new—to New Mexico, anyway—material. Bricks had several advantages over adobe: they could be made faster, they weathered better, and they produced buildings more like the ones back home.

Courtesy Silver City Museum

David Abraham Family
Nineteenth century

David Abraham arrived in southwestern New Mexico in the late 1860s, settling in Silver City in 1871 to become a pillar of the community.

Abraham died in Silver City in 1894, and the obituary notice indicates, "In 1873 he applied for and obtained the first patent to a mining claim ever issued for a claim in New Mexico. He built several substantial business structures while he engaged in real estate and mining transactions, as well as the mercantile business."

The above photograph shows David holding Hyman in his right arm and Louie in his left arm, Jake and Abe are standing, his wife, Esther, is sitting holding Sarah, Anna is standing, Phoebe is seated holding Sam.

Courtesy Silver City Museum

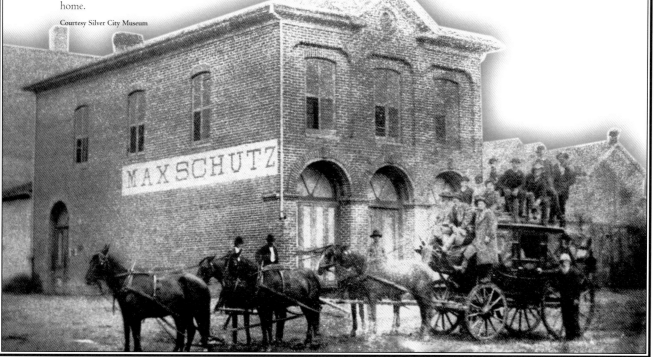

Sigmund Lindauer

c. 1893

Courtesy Deming Luna Mimbres Museum

Lindauer Receipt and Advertisement

n.d.

Eventually Sigmund Lindauer moved his mercantile operation from Silver City to Deming, New Mexico. Besides merchandising, Sigmund also was involved in the cattle business and some farming. He served as treasurer of Grant County in 1888 and as a delegate in the Populist Party.

Courtesy Deming Luna Mimbres Museum

S. Lindauer & Co. Storefront

c. 1874

Sigmund Lindauer arrived in Silver City in 1872, having heard of a mining discovery in southwestern New Mexico. In the mid-1870s he opened a store in Georgetown, a booming silver camp.

Courtesy Deming Luna Mimbres Museum

Political Pioneers, Pioneering Ventures

In the early 1900s the Jewish community became stronger, making its mark in politics in southern New Mexico, where its members also pioneered in agriculture and international trade.

Louis Freudenthal became well known in southern New Mexico politics. Samuel Klein served as mayor of Las Cruces. Sigmund and Julius Moise each served as mayor of Santa Rosa. Henry Jaffa, the first mayor of Albuquerque, and Mike Mandell, the second, were prominent members of the Jewish community.

Louis Ravel, a Lithuanian immigrant and New Mexico businessman, was another prominent member, who became mayor of Columbus. There, he and his brother survived a raid by Pancho Villa's soldiers.

Henry Jaffa
n.d.

Albuquerque's first mayor

Mike Mandell
ca. 1900

Albuquerque's second mayor

Courtesy Center of Southwest Research,
University of New Mexico, Neg. No.
1978.050.248

Columbus in Ruins
1916

Smoking ruins of Columbus, raided by Pancho Villa,
March 1916

Museum of New Mexico, Neg. No. 5805

Ceremonial Dance at Acoma Pueblo
1883

far left: Solomon Bibo.

Museum of New Mexico, Neg. No. 16383

By 1900, many Jewish citizens had become involved in local politics. No example was more unusual than that of trader Solomon Bibo, who was elected governor of Acoma Pueblo at least three times.

Law and politics

left background: **Solomon Spiegelberg**
1880–1884

Appointed to the Santa Fe County Commission in the 1870s, Solomon Spiegelberg was elected to the County Board in 1880 and later became its president.

Museum of New Mexico, Neg. No. 11024°

Bernard Seligman
n.d.

Bernard Seligman served as a member of the Territorial House from Santa Fe County in 1880. Later, he was appointed to the Office of Territorial Treasurer.

Museum of New Mexico, Neg. No. 11018

Louis Ilfeld and Anna Staab celebrated Washinton's birthday (see page 7)

I n the early territorial days, New Mexico was a rough part of the West, where Mexican cultural traditions clashed with newcomers' values, and where gambling, alcohol, and other dangers involved both natives and recent arrivals. Young Jewish immigrants were as vulnerable to violence as anyone else. The notorious gang of outlaw "Black Jack" Ketchum, for instance, murdered Levi Herzstein in Mora County in 1896.

Social and cultural institutions, particularly in Santa Fe, provided some order for the burgeoning population. As Jewish business fortunes grew throughout the 1860s and 1870s, their grand, architecturally stylish homes became centers of the region's social and cultural activity. Music and the arts were expressions of their European backgrounds. Rosalia Hersch had her piano carried across the Santa Fe Trail to Santa Fe. Jacob Amberg's wife composed music and gave piano lessons. Flora Spiegelberg played Chopin on the piano at "musicale" evenings in her home.

Women were also active outside their homes. For instance, Elizabeth Nordhaus reminisces about her mother in Albuquerque: "Mother had become involved in child welfare work and served on the State Department of Public Welfare under three governors. . . . She also kept busy finding homes for unwanted or orphaned children."

The Jewish community addressed their public identity through participation in secular organizations, such as Masonic lodges, Order of Odd Fellows lodges, the Ladies Benevolent Society, and the Germania Club (1878). In line with their civil organization involvement, some early Jewish pioneers also became founders, donors, and active members of the Historical Society of New Mexico, founded in 1859. Over the decades many Jewish men gravitated toward these groups. The Masons, having a history of respect for all religious beliefs, welcomed Jewish pioneers into their lodges throughout the state. This fraternal organization helped form bonds of friendship, trust, and individual respect that extended into the civic, social, and business activities, and developing institutions in New Mexico communities. Many of the Jewish pioneers were lifelong Masons, and Jewish participation in Masonic lodges was evident throughout the state. A booklet of "By-Laws for the Santa Fe Chapter" lists a significant number of Jewish members, including the Spiegelbergs, Albert Elsberg, and Jacob Amberg. Another member was Hyman Abraham, whose father, David Abraham, was also a Mason and highly respected by the community. For a time, the father served as probate judge for Grant County and as treasurer for the town of Silver City.

Interaction, often cordial, existed between Jewish citizens and their neighbors, despite differences of religion and/or ethnic background. Apparent were such affiliations between Santa Fe's Spiegelberg and Staab families and Archbishop Jean Baptiste Lamy. The somewhat folkloristic anecdote about the Tetragrammaton in Santa Fe only confirms these relationships. Above the entrance to St. Francis Cathedral are the four consonants of the ancient Hebrew name for God—known as the Tetragrammaton—inscribed within a triangle, a common Christian symbol for the Trinity. It's difficult to know whether Archbishop Jean Baptiste Lamy simply intended this inscription as a traditional Christian symbol, or if he had it added in honor of his friendship with Santa Fe's Jewish community and its generous contributions toward cathedral construction costs. Elizabeth Nordhaus remembers that, "in 1967 Grandfather Staab was posthumously honored at the Annual Conference of Christians and Jews for his help in building the Cathedral in Santa Fe. On three different occasions Grandfather loaned money to construct the church. When the mortgage came due, the Archbishop announced sadly that he could not repay the loan. Grandfather tore up the papers, and in gratitude, the Archbishop put the Hebrew inscription on the door of the cathedral and there you will find it when you go to Santa Fe."

On another occasion, Jewish pioneer Bernard Seligman won in a raffle a wool tapestry made by the Catholic Sisters of Loretto. With his brother, Sigmund, he established Seligman Brothers in 1862. Bernard Seligman married Frances Nusbaum, daughter of John Nusbaum, who had founded one of America's first department stores in Harrisburg, Pennsylvania.

The Staabs and their mansion on Palace Avenue figured prominently in Santa Fe social life. Attended by military and civilian dignitaries, governors, justices, visiting notables, and officers of high rank, these Staab gatherings made life at Fort Marcy and in Santa Fe preferable to that in many of the great regimental posts of the Far West. In her reminiscences Elizabeth Nordhaus recollects that "my Aunt Delia told us of the interesting life in Santa Fe in those days. There were few well-educated girls in the community, and as the army moved in and out, they were in great demand at the many dances, balls and riding parties."

Social activities were not restricted to Santa Fe or Albuquerque. David Remley notes that "Yetta Kohn was La Cinta's unofficial social director, entertaining royally any visitor who may chance to pass her threshold. Her ferry was a wooden flatboat that she pulled back and forth across the Canadian by a rope attached to both banks."

It is not surprising that Louis Hommel liked to think that the "Canadian River region was becoming metropolitan," considering that on several social occasions nearby residences served imported Bordeaux wine and seven-course dinners including oyster soup, chicken broth with rice, roast "joints" of mutton with caper sauce, beef with cranberry sauce, fricassee of chicken "Alamande," boned turkey, and pâté de fois gras.

Gentile Mary Lillie May married Dirk Seligman, who was born in Berlin in 1863. He arrived looking for opportunities in the Las Cruces area in 1889, and with the May family entered into a partnership managing the dry goods side of the store. Herman Ilfeld, the first of the Ilfeld brothers to arrive in New Mexico, became a partner in the mercantile firm of Elsberg & Amberg in the 1860s.

Jacob Amberg is himself an example of the familial as well as interpersonal and mercantile connections of these early pioneers. After prospecting silver claims in Piños Altos by Silver City, he joined forces in 1855 with Gustave Elsberg, one of the first Jewish merchants in Westport, Kansas. A year later Elsberg and Amberg moved down the Santa Fe Trail to Santa Fe. The firm financed Adolph Letcher in his Taos business venture, A. Letcher & Co. There eighteen-year-old Charles Ilfeld initially worked as a clerk. When he later became a partner, Ilfeld purchased Letcher's share of the business and established a company bearing his name in Las Vegas. The Ilfelds were cousins of Elsberg and Amberg.

Flora and Willi Spiegelberg also had a close friendship with Governor Lew Wallace, who was writing parts of *Ben Hur* while living in the Palace of the Governors. In her 1937 unpublished memoir *Reminiscences of a Jewish Bride of the Santa Fe Trail*, Flora recalls:

> The large window at the old El Palacio Real is still shown to tourists where Governor Wallace used to sit after office hours and work on his manuscript *Ben Hur*. One day as I passed I looked in the window and bowed good morning. The Governor beckoned to me to come in, he said, "Mrs. Spiegelberg, I have just wrapped up my manuscript of *Ben Hur*, to forward to my publisher, do you think it is worth the expressage?" For a moment I stared at him then quickly replied, "My dear Governor, judging by the success of your book, *The Prince of Peace*, I'd gladly pay the express charges if you agree to divide the royalties with me?" He smiled, saying, "I will consider your offer" and I wished him good luck. It has been said that the royalties from the book *Ben Hur*, the play and the film amounted to a million dollars. I often joked with him about my offer, and how wise he was not to accept it."

Her intellectual curiosity and cosmopolitan aura made Flora one of Santa Fe's social leaders. She was also a community pillar through her active concerns for education, religion, and other civic needs.

After 1880 and the coming of the railroad, New Mexican society underwent a period of rapid social change. Jewish pioneers lived in settlements along the expanding rail and in mining camps. They became involved in many social services and civic projects, such as forming and staffing volunteer fire departments, organizing civic drives, and planting shade trees. They helped create new education and service organiza-

Isaacs Store Float

July 4, 1912

At an Independence Day parade in Clayton

Courtesy Isaacs Family Collection, Clayton

tions, and served on the boards of regents for the Las Vegas Normal School (later, New Mexico Highlands University) and the New Mexico Military Institute in Roswell. In Santa Fe Jewish pioneers revived the Historical Society of New Mexico, located in the Palace of the Governors.

Much that visitors to New Mexico viewed as primitive, backward, and foreign—customs, traditions, architecture, road conditions, to name but a few—became the substance of everyday life for the Jewish settlers. The experiences that shaped the pioneers' lives—their endeavors to build communities, schools, and other social institutions—characterized the decades of the state's long struggle to join the Union. From the social and cultural centers of Santa Fe and Las Vegas, to the lonely lives of rural Jewish pioneers on railroad, mining, and cattle frontiers, they entered wholeheartedly into the social development of the land they called home.

Civic and Social Organizations

With a history of respect for all religious beliefs, the Masons welcomed Jewish pioneers into lodges throughout New Mexico. The bonds of friendship, trust, and respect for the individual forged within this fraternal organization extended outside lodge meetings, strengthening the civic, social, and business activities, and developing institutions of New Mexico communities. Many of the Jewish pioneers were dedicated lifelong Masons.

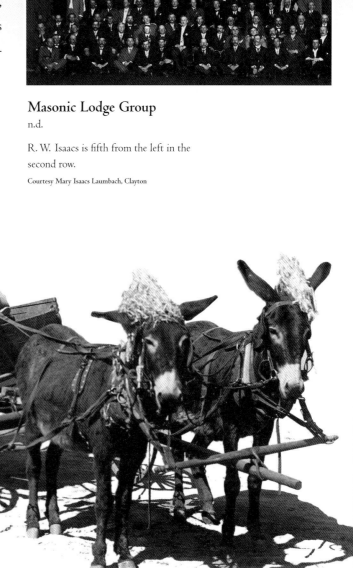

Masonic Lodge Group
n.d.

R. W. Isaacs is fifth from the left in the second row.

Courtesy Mary Isaacs Laumbach, Clayton

Shriners, in Raton
1910

R. W. Isaacs in cap and glasses
Courtesy R. W. Isaacs Family, Clayton

Jacob Wertheim

1914

Jacob Wertheim was a member of the Tucumcari Masonic Lodge.

Courtesy Tucumcari Masonic Lodge

The Historical Society.

According to announcement a meeting was held yesterday afternoon for the purpose of re-organizing the Historical Society of New Mexico.

General H. M. Atkinson was called on to preside, and Captain Louis Felsenthal was made secretary of the meeting.

By request of Secretary Ritch the secretary stated the object of the meeting.

The constitution of the old society, organized just twenty one years ago, was read by the secretary and submitted to the meeting for adoption as the constitution of the society in the future. After a few slight alterations it was adopted and signed by H. M. Atkinson, Louis Felsenthal, David J. Miller, Samuel Ellison, W. G. Ritch, Sol. Spiegelberg, L. Bradford Prince, H. O. Ladd, and C. A. Woodruff.

On motion the meeting then adjourned till the last Friday in January, when a permanent organization will be effected

Alex Goldenberg of Tucumcari

n. d.

Courtesy Tucumcari Masonic Lodge

left: **Article from the Daily New Mexican**

December 28, 1880 (enlarged detail)

Louis Felsenthal and Solomon Spiegelberg are listed among the nine men who reorganized the Historical Society of New Mexico in 1880.

Courtesy Fray Angélico Chavez Library Palace of the Governors

Souvenir Bell

1897

Embossed: "To Chas. Ilfeld from Adolph Letcher/
A Happy New Year 1897"

Charles Ilfeld's association with Adolph Letcher proved to be
a productive learning experience. Young Ilfeld worked as a clerk for
Letcher in Taos for two years in the late 1860s. When opportunities
blossomed in Las Vegas, the two loaded their merchandise on seventy-
five burros and moved there to set up the business as A. Letcher and
Company, as partners.

Palace of the Governors Collections (4111/45)

Silver Locket

c. 1880

Engraved with "H. S. I." for Helen S. Ilfeld

Palace of the Governors Collections (1055/45)

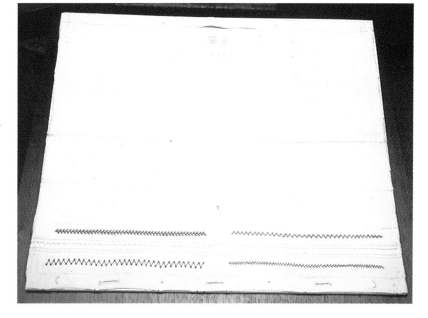

Child's Sampler

1885

"This sampler represents my first lessons in rudimen-
tary sewing while attending Mme. Froehlich's private
school for girls in New York in the year 1885."

—Helen S. Ilfeld

Palace of the Governors Collections (1041/45)

Candlesticks

c. 1900

These candlesticks belonged to Anna Freudenthal of Las Cruces.

On loan from Ann F. Ramenofsky
(Anna's great-granddaughter), Albuquerque

Soup Tureen

c. 1900

This bowl belonged to Wagon Mound resident Theresa Vorenberg, who used it on the many occasions when she entertained in her home.

Gift of Jeanette Werthheim Sparks, granddaughter of
Theresa Vorenberg, Carlsbad

Tea Service

c. 1860s

Bernard Seligman married Frances Nusbaum, daughter of John Nusbaum, founder of one of the first department stores in America, in Harrisburg, Pennsylvania. This sterling silver tea set made by the Gorham Company belonged to the couple. Their initials appear on all of these pieces.

Palace of the Governors Collections
(9548/45, 9554/45)

Serving Pieces

1874

These sterling silver pieces were given to Flora and Willi Spiegelberg for their 1874 wedding in Nuremberg. They were used in their Santa Fe home on East Palace Avenue until their departure for New York in the 1890s. The fish knife and serving spoon were patented in 1868 by Starr and Marcus. The cake service has "W. S." (Willi Spiegelberg) engraved on the bottom of the handle.

On loan from Felix and Susan (Spiegelberg) Warburg,
San Francisco, California

Soup Tureen

n.d.

This family heirloom was brought by wagon from Fort Leavenworth, Kansas, over the Santa Fe Trail to Las Vegas by the Goldsmith family. It belonged to Lena Goldsmith before her marriage to Morris Herzstein, a member of another prominent New Mexico Jewish merchant family.

On loan from Mr. and Mrs. Mortimer H. Herzstein,
San Francisco, California

Moustache Cup and Saucer

n.d.

These items belonged to Bernard Seligman.

Palace of the Governors Collections (9554/45a,b)

Albuquerque Browns Baseball Club

c. 1900

Mike Mandell, Albuquerque's second mayor, is second from
right in middle row.

Courtesy Center of Southwest Research, University of New Mexico, Neg. No.
0001190438

left: **Helenita Zeckendorf**

c. 1874

Helenita Zeckendorf was one of Aaron and Mathilda Zeckendorf's three children.

Courtesy Harold and Iris Masback, White Plains, New York

George Washington Birthday Party

February 22, 1899

Louis Ilfeld and Anna Staab Ilfeld celebrated George Washington's
birthday at a party given for their three children at the San Felipe
Hotel in Old Town, Albuquerque.

Courtesy Betty-Mae Hartman, Albuquerque

right: **Hugo Aaron Zeckendorf**
c. 1866

In 1854 Hugo's father, Aaron Zeckendorf, founded A. & L. Zeckendorf & Co. in Santa Fe.

Courtesy Harold & Iris Masback, White Plains, New York

Flora Spiegelberg and Daughters
1888

Betty and Rose with their mother, in front of their home on
Palace Avenue in Santa Fe.

Courtesy Felix and Susan (Spiegelberg) Warburg, San Francisco, California

Bernice Bacharach

n.d.

Courtesy New Mexico Jewish
Historical Society,
New Mexico State Records
Center and Archives

Bacharach Family Portrait

n.d.

lower left Henriette Ilfeld; *upper left:* Bertha Spiegelberg; *upper right:* Belle Bacharach; *lower right:* Soloman Jacob Spiegelberg and Isaac Bacharach

Courtesy New Mexico Jewish Historical Society,
New Mexico State Records Center and Archives

Herman "Ike" Bacharach

n.d.

Courtesy New Mexico Jewish Historical Society,
New Mexico State Records Center and Archives

**Watercolor Painting
by Herman I. Bacharach**

n.d.

Courtesy New Mexico Jewish Historical Society,
New Mexico State Records Center and Archives

"A Happy New Year"

1897

New Mexico's Jewish merchants and their families celebrated the High Holy Days with enthusiasm.

On loan from Kit Carson Historical Museum, Weimer Collection, Taos

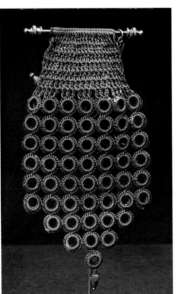

Lorgnette Eyeglasses, Sampler, and Brooch

Late nineteenth century

Helen Schutz Ilfeld, second wife of Noa Ilfeld, owned and donated these and other family mementos to the Historical Society of New Mexico in 1953. The sampler was made by her in 1885; the brooch came from Toledo, Spain.

Palace of the Governors Collections (1039/45, 1053/45, 1041/45, 1058/45, 1055/45)

Watch Fob and Coin Purse

Late nineteenth century

This crocheted and beaded watch fob and coin purse were made by Elise Apflebaum Rosenwald, a native of Fürth, Germany. She was married to Las Vegas merchant Emanuel Rosenwald. Shortly after their wedding in 1872, Mr. Rosenwald took his bride to live in Las Vegas. She had been a "needle woman" before their marriage.

Palace of the Governors Collections (443/45)

**Julia Schuster Staab, wife of
Abraham Staab**
n.d.

Courtesy Betty-Mae Hartman, Albuquerque

**Abraham Staab, prominent Santa Fe
merchant**
n.d.

Courtesy Betty-Mae Hartman, Albuquerque

**The Staab Mansion
Santa Fe**
n.d.

*The Staab mansion on Palace Avenue played prominently [in Santa Fe social
life]. Attended by dignitaries, military and civilian, governors, justices, visiting
notables and officers of high rank, these entertainments made life at Fort Marcy
and old Santa Fe preferable to that in many of the great regimental posts of the
far west.*

—Ralph E. Twitchell,
Old Santa Fe: The Story of New Mexico's Ancient Capital

*Summers were pretty hot in Albuquerque, so the family spent most of them at the Staab house in Santa Fe.
The move involved a considerable amount of preparation, including the shipping of two cows, as the milk
supply in Santa Fe was not the best.*

—Beatrice Ilfeld Meyer,
Don Luis Ilfeld: Memories of His Daughters

*Mother was 35 when she married
Father. Fortunately Grandfather
approved.*

—Elizabeth Nordhaus Minces,
The Family: Early Days in New Mexico

Elizabeth Minces Staab
n.d.
Courtesy Nancy M. Paxton, Albuquerque

Bertha was decades ahead of her time when she omitted the word 'obey' from her wedding vows. The ceremony in 1907 to Max Nordhaus meant the end of her residency in Santa Fe. They moved to Albuquerque where she became a great leader in philanthropic work and helped promote the first child labor laws in New Mexico.

—Marian Meyer,
*Santa Fe's Fifteen Club:
A Century of Literary Women*

Bertha Staab Nordhaus

c. 1895

Bertha Staab Nordhaus was the daughter of Abraham Staab and the wife of Max Nordhaus.

Courtesy Nancy M. Paxton, Albuquerque

We lived in a three-story house with basement on the corner of 12th and Central. It was a wonderful place in which to grow up. Sunday noon dinner was a very formal affair with a three or four course meal and almost never fewer than twelve people. Ranchers, business associates, strangers from the East who had letters of introduction from mutual friends or single persons without families were always included.

Mother had become involved in child welfare work and served on the State Department of Public Welfare under three governors . . . . She also kept busy finding homes for unwanted or orphaned children.

Father spent much of his time visiting the country stores and ranches, seeking room and board wherever he could find it. He traveled by horse and buggy, eating pork and beans with the sheepherders, sometimes sharing a bed with a member of the family, or seeking shelter in one of the houses of the old Spanish families . . . .

My Aunt Delia told us of the interesting life in Santa Fe in those days. There were few well-educated girls in the community, and as the army moved in and out, they were in great demand at the many dances, balls and riding parties. Mother often served as hostess for Governor Hagerman, a bachelor, and was included in a large group that went to the Hopi Snake Dances—six days by wagon and horseback to get there.

—Elizabeth Nordhaus Minces,
The Family: Early Days in New Mexico

The Staab-Nordhaus Family

c. 1915

Max Nordhaus and Bertha Staab married and had three children. They are pictured here at their home at 12th and Central, Albuquerque. *standing:* Maxine and Max; *seated:* Elizabeth, Bertha, and Robert.

Courtesy Nancy M. Paxton, Albuquerque

Known Jewish Pioneer Women in New Mexico

Abrams, Flora (Mrs. Nathan Bibo)

Abrams, ? (Mrs. Joseph Bibo)

Apflebaum, Elise (Mrs. Emanuel Rosenwald),
  b. Fürth, Bavaria

Bacharach, Hannah (Mrs. Felix Strausse)

Bibo, Clara (Mrs. Herman Block)

Bibo, Irma (Mrs. Ben Floersheim)

Bibo, Lina (Mrs. Isadore Weiss)

Bibo, Viola (Mrs. Sidney Rosenwald)

Biernbaum, Rachel
  (the first Mrs. Benjamin Lowenstein)

Block, Blanche (Mrs. Julius Seligman)

Block, Lucille (Mrs. Carl Seligman)

Block, Meta (Mrs. Sigfried Seligman)

Blumenthal, Emma (Mrs. Solomon Floersheim)

Eichholz, Johanna (Mrs. Max Schuster)

Eichholz, Paula (Mrs. Ludwig Kempenich),
  b. Düsseldorf, Rhineland

Elsberg, Bertha (Mrs. ? Beuthner),
  b. Iserlohn, Germany

Ferse, Bertha (Mrs. Alexander Gusdorf)

Florence, Rachel (Mrs. Friedrich Salsbury)

Freudenthal, Anna (Mrs. Isadore Solomon),
  b. Posen, Prussian Poland

Gold, Maggie (Mrs. Hyman Rinaldo,
  her second husband), *b. Poland*

Goldsmit, Mathilda (Mrs. Aaron Zeckendorf), b. Hanover, Germany

Goldsmith, Bertha (Mrs. Sigmund Lindauer)

Goldsmith, Lena (Mrs. Morris Herzstein)

Goldsmith, Yetta (Mrs. Samuel Kohn), *b. Bavaria*

Gottleib, Julie (Mrs. Phillip Strausse)

Grunsfeld, Sallie (Mrs. Albert Eiseman)

Harris, Theresa (Mrs. Simon Vorenberg),
  b. Philadelphia

Herschberg, Rosalia (Mrs. Joseph Hersch),
  b. Prussian Poland

Hoffelmann, Lena G. (Mrs. Frank O. Kihlberg)

Hyman, Mabel (Mrs. Alfred Kempenich)

Ilfeld, Elizabeth (Mrs. Samuel Salsbury)

Jackson, Phoebe
  (the second Mrs. Moses Aaron Gold)

Jaffa, Ella (Mrs. Leo J. Strauss)

Kempenich, Elsie (Mrs. Julius Gans)

Klein, Juli (Mrs. Carl Harberg)

Kohn, Belle (Mrs. Albert Calish)

Langerman, Flora (Mrs. Willie Spiegelberg),
  b. New York City

Lehmann, Veronica (Mrs. Herman Obermayer)

Leopold, Carrie (Mrs. Lehman Spiegelberg)

Lesinsky, Mathilda (Mrs. Henry Lesinsky)

Lesinsky, Nellie (Mrs. Max Schutz)

Leventrill, Mathilda (Mrs. Louis Zeckendorf)

Levisohn, Bona (Mrs. Joseph Rosenwald)

Lowenbien, Wilhemina (Mrs. Jacob Amberg),
  b. Szegedin, Hungary

Lowendahl, Jenie (Mrs. Abraham Kempenich)

Lowitsky, Jennie (Mrs. Sol Lowitsky)

Mack, Pauline (Mrs. Samuel Bibo)

Nordhaus, Adele (Mrs. Charles Ilfeld),
  b. Paderhorn, Westphalia, Bavaria

Nordhaus, Fanny (Mrs. Aaron Schutz),
  b. Paderhorn, Westphalia, Bavaria

Nusbaum, Frances (Mrs. Bernard Seligman),
  b. Philadelphia

Ochs, Fanny (Mrs. Zadoc Staab)

Oppenheim, Bessie (Mrs. Henry Jaffa)

Rosenwald, Helene (Mrs. Jacob Goldsmith)

Rosenwald, Julia (Mrs. Phillip Strausse)

Salsbury, Augusta (Mrs. Marcus Jacob Brunswick),
  b. New York

Salsbury, Bertha (Mrs. Henry Biernbaum)

Salsbury, Bertha (Mrs. Herman Wedeles)

Salsbury, Ernestine (Mrs. Jacob Gusdorf)

Scholand, Emilie Fritz (Mrs. David Abraham)

Schuster, Julia (Mrs. Abe Staab)

Schuster, Rose (Mrs. Samuel Danoff)

Seligman, Betty (Mrs. Levi Spiegelberg)

Spiegelberg, Minna (Mrs. Alfred Grunsfeld),
  b. Natzungen, Westphalia

Spiro, Sara (Mrs. Henry Grant),
  b. Poland

Staab, Adela (Mrs. Louis Baer)

Staab, Anna (Mrs. Louis Ilfeld)

Staab, Sophia (Mrs. Joseph Gusdorf)

Steinhart, Kathie (Mrs. Sol J. Spiegelberg)

Stern, Bertha (the first Mrs. Jacob Regensberg)

Strauss, Esther (Mrs. Nathan Jaffa)

Strauss, Millie (Mrs. Joseph Jaffa)

Strauss, Rose (the second Mrs. Benjamin Lowenstein)

Uhlfelder, Elise (Mrs. Aaron Goldsmith and/or
  Mrs. Emanuel Aaron Rosenwald),
  b. Regensberg, Germany

Vigdorovici, Haia Etel (Mrs. Morris Bell),
  b. Jassy, Romania

Weisl, ? (Mrs. Charles Lesinsky)

Weisskoph, Elizabeth (Mrs. Emil Bibo),
  b. Mallinetz, Bohemia, Austria

Wells, Rosella (Mrs. Thomas Levy)

Wertheim, Emma (Mrs. Henry Goldenburg),
  b. Helmarshausen, Hesse Kassel

Wertheim, Henrietta (Mrs. Alex Goldenburg),
  b. Helmarshausen, Hesse Kassel

Jewish Women of Mora

c. 1885

A group photograph of women, mostly unidentified, who were the wives of local Jewish merchants and who appear to have formed a sewing society.

Courtesy Kit Carson Historical Museum, Weimer Collection, Taos, Neg. No. 78.24.58

Beaded Needlepoint

n.d.

Anna Freudenthal stitched this in the Berlin style. This work hung in the family hotel in Solomonville, Arizona, a town named for Anna's husband, Isidor Solomon.

On loan from Ann F. Ramenofsky, Albuquerque

Wedding Shoes

1898

Belle Ilfeld wore these satin shoes when she married Isaac Bacharach on November 9, 1898. The ceremony was performed by Rabbi B. A. Bonheim of Las Vegas. The local newspaper featured a column on the wedding noting that, "The ceremony was an impressive and solemn ritual of the Jewish faith, for if there is any people who hold the bonds of matrimony a sacred thing, it is the Jewish people. . . ."

Palace of the Governors Collections (10935/45, 10937/45)

Without established religious institutions, the Jews of New Mexico often found it challenging to observe their religion in a formal sense prior to 1880. Although the state may not have been the most fertile ground for formal religious practices, it could be argued that this was actually an attraction for many of the German Jewish immigrants who preferred a secular religion to the Orthodox faith of dietary restrictions and literal readings of sacred texts. The American doctrine of separation of church and state certainly assisted in this secularization of the Jewish religion.

The Jews did, however, celebrate the High Holy Days (Rosh Hashanah [Jewish New Year] and Yom Kippur) and bar mitzvahs in homes and Masonic lodges. Flora Spiegelberg, wife of Santa Fe Mayor Willi Spiegelberg, recalls in her memoir that Archbishop Jean Baptiste Lamy sent gifts of fruit and flowers from his garden to the tiny Jewish community at celebrations of Rosh Hashanah and Passover. The first Yom Kippur in New Mexico was observed in 1860 at the home of Betty Spiegelberg.

Many pioneers retained their Jewish identity, despite their isolation and the rigors of their lives. In isolated New Mexico towns, for instance, individual families managed to maintain their Jewish customs, as Emma Vorenberg Wertheim recalls in her unpublished memoir of growing up in Cleveland, a tiny town outside Mora, where her father ran a general store: "At the time [1889] there were only two white families in Cleveland: the Cassidys, who were Catholic, and the Vorenbergs. Most of the people in that sparsely settled community were settlers of Mexican-American descent. . . . My mother was a true 'mother of Israel.' She baked Shabbas bread each Friday, and every Friday night we had a real Shabbas dinner, with prayer at the table and the blessings over the candles, the wine and the bread. We always practiced Judaism in our home, and it is remarkable that we remained Jewish in this isolated little community where we were the only family of our faith."

Those in far-flung towns would travel considerable distances to participate in religious services. Itinerant practitioners came from as far away as Denver for other observances, such as the circumcision of newborn sons.

From the 1870s onward, the early pattern of strong, extended families in which the first pioneers lived, worked, and practiced their Judaism gradually began to change. With marriage and children, new families emerged and began to reshape the Jewish way of life. The years between 1880 and 1914 proved to be the time when Jewish religious institutions were created in New Mexico. Newcomers arrived in greater numbers, and the original social composition of the Jewish population underwent transformation. The birth of the next generation raised vital issues about their religious education.

The American Reform tradition, which had its roots in Germany and was based in Cincinnati, Ohio, was strong among Jewish pioneers in the western states. Emphasizing individual autonomy and advocating pluralism, this movement stood on fertile ground in the West. It enabled the Jews to adapt to the frontier life while preserving tradition, and to embrace New Mexico's diversity while asserting commonality. Many of the early rabbis in the West were either students or graduates of the Rabbinical School founded in Cincinnati or were influenced by the 1885 Pittsburgh Platform, which formalized the practices and thoughts of this Reform Movement.

Many young Jewish men who came to New Mexico in the early wave of pioneers went to great lengths to seek marriageable Jewish women. They returned to eastern cities or even to Europe, often to find traditionally arranged marriages with distant relatives or family friends. Others—mainly those who lived in isolated areas without any members of their faith nearby—sometimes chose intermarriage with Hispanic New Mexican or Indian women, a course that often resulted in the husband's assimilation.

By the 1880s some communities began formal congregations, yet many more remained without a temple. Santa Fe had no congregation, which may have been due to its deteriorating economic conditions and the fact that some of its prominent Jewish citizens had returned to the East. In other small towns during this period, a handful of Jews created less formal congregations. In Roswell, for example, such an informal group came into existence in 1903.

Many of these more recent settlers came from Eastern Europe with established Orthodox beliefs. Their religion contrasted to the largely Reform background of the earlier pioneers. Nevertheless, successful efforts to organize in more formal ways were undertaken. In the early 1880s Albuquerque Jews founded a chapter of B'nai B'rith, a fraternal and mutual-aid organization. Simultaneously three Reform temples were built in the area: Congregation Montefiore declared itself in 1884 and built Temple Montefiore in Las Vegas in 1886; Temple Aaron was founded in Trinidad, Colorado, in 1883 and constructed a temple in 1889; Congregation Albert in Albuquerque was formed in 1897 and completed Temple Albert two years later.

Congregation Montefiore was the earliest formal organization of Jews in New Mexico. Forty years after the first Jewish pioneers arrived in New Mexico Territory, on September 26, 1886, the congregation dedicated New Mexico's first Jewish temple. According to a building committee report, the congregation raised the $2,400 needed for construction through pledges of $100 to $150, including contributions from many non-Jewish well-wishers. Merchant Charles Ilfeld purchased for the congregation the lot at 9th Street and Douglas Avenue for $640. The congregation named itself for the nineteenth-century Jewish philanthropist Sir Moses Montefiore. Rev. Dr. Joseph Glueck, affiliated with the Union of American Hebrew Congregations (Reform Judaism), arrived from Owenboro, Kentucky, to serve as the first rabbi both for the congregation and for the entire state. The congregation had thirty-two charter members; N. S. Rosenthal served as first president. At its height around 1900, as many as 200 congregants represented between seventy and seventy-five families. Members from outlying areas such as Wagon Mound, Tucumcari, and Santa Rosa traveled great distances to attend services, held twice a week.

Shortly after the congregation was established, other Jewish associations coalesced in Las Vegas. Congregation Montefiore Cemetery was founded on February 7, 1888, on the same grounds as the Las Vegas Masonic Cemetery. In 1902 the J. E. Rosenwald Lodge No. 545 of B'nai B'rith was founded. Two years later the Hebrew Ladies Benevolent Society began, eventually transforming into the Council of Jewish Women in 1920. Membership started to decline after the World War I era and, with too few members to maintain the building, it was sold in 1957.

Just across the territorial border, in Trinidad, Colorado, another Jewish congregation organized formally. During the late nineteenth and early twentieth centuries, Trinidad was a bustling commercial center. Its German Jewish merchants provided miners with food, clothing, and supplies. In 1872 the small Jewish community celebrated its first Rosh Hashanah. Seven years later a B'nai B'rith lodge was formed, and on July 23, 1883, seventeen men joined together as the Israelites of Trinidad. They moved forward with plans to build a synagogue, which they named Temple Aaron, after the father of the three merchant Jaffa brothers. The Ladies' Auxiliary was formed in 1889 and promptly started holding bake sales to raise as much as possible of the $12,500 needed to build the temple.

The traditional-looking, onion-domed Reform synagogue was built in 1889 by one of the region's preeminent architects, Isaac Hamilton Rapp, who went on to become a primary creator of the "Santa Fe Style." The two-story, red-brick and pink sandstone building is a hybrid of Victorian and Moorish designs. From the Tiffany-style stained-glass windows to the gleaming pine woodwork, the temple was furnished with the best available materials. A pipe organ was brought in by wagon.

Once built, Temple Aaron served a wide community of Jewish pioneers scattered throughout northeastern New Mexico and southern Colorado. Members traveled from the railroad town of Clayton and the gold-mine boom town of Elizabethtown to participate in services. Leopold Freudenthal served as a rabbi from 1889 until his death in 1916. Situated on its original location, Temple Aaron remains the oldest continuously operating synagogue in Colorado.

Other congregations were established in New Mexico's largest city. On September 26, 1897, Temple Albert was founded in Albuquerque. With the arrival of the railroad, the community of German-speaking Reform Jewish pioneers continued to experience healthy growth. The temple derived its name through an auction. Alfred Grunsfeld, who in 1876 had the first bar mitzvah in New Mexico, made the winning bid to have the temple named for his father. Albuquerque's social and political leaders became early supporters of

Temple Albert. Henry N. Jaffa became the congregation's first president, and Mike Mandell was an active member of the young congregation. The official dedication of the domed temple took place on September 15, 1900. By that time, Congregation Albert had fifty members, including some from Bernalillo and other communities.

The arrival in Albuquerque of eastern European Jewish pioneers with Orthodox beliefs eventually resulted in the establishment of Congregation B'nai Israel, incorporated in 1920. As early as 1915, this small community held services in private homes and other informal gathering places. During the 1920s, leaders of Congregation B'nai Israel supported the Zionist Organization of America in the effort to establish a Jewish homeland in Palestine. By the time the congregation laid the cornerstone for a building at Coal and Cedar Avenues in 1941, its affiliation had become Conservative. It remains to this day in its home at Washington Street and Indian School Road.

The years between 1880 and 1914 proved to be the time when Jewish religious institutions were created in New Mexico. Newcomers arrived in greater numbers and the original social composition of the Jewish population underwent transformation. The birth of the next generation raised vital issues about their religious education.

Laying the Cornerstone

Temple Albert, Albuquerque, September 3, 1899

Courtesy Albuquerque Museum, Milner Studio Collection, Neg. No. 1992 005 503

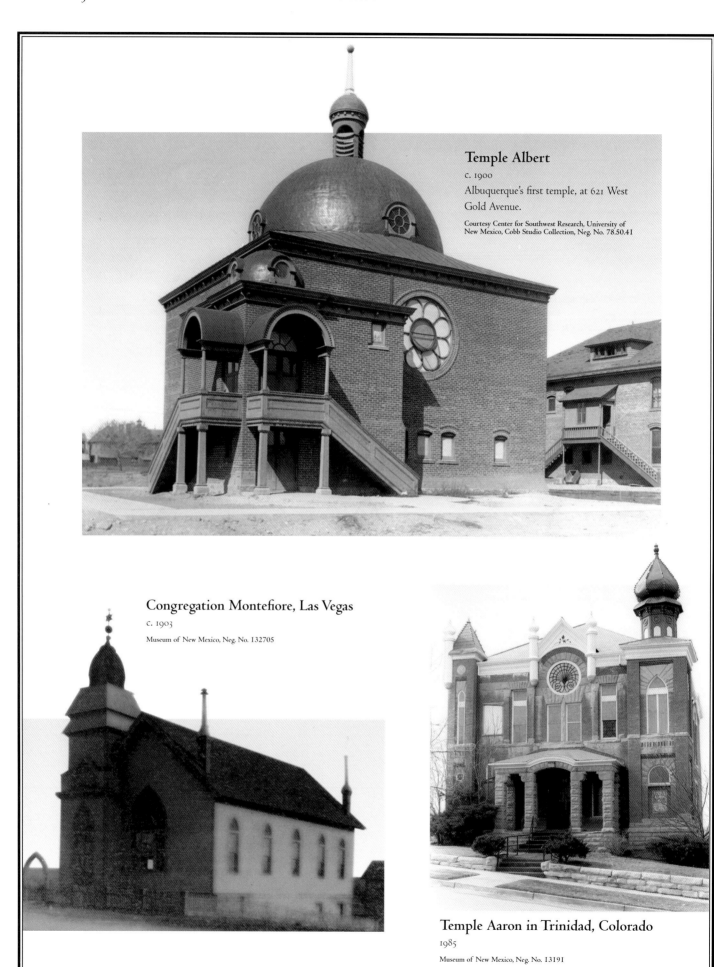

Temple Albert

c. 1900

Albuquerque's first temple, at 621 West Gold Avenue.

Courtesy Center for Southwest Research, University of New Mexico, Cobb Studio Collection, Neg. No. 78.50.41

Congregation Montefiore, Las Vegas

c. 1903

Museum of New Mexico, Neg. No. 132705

Temple Aaron in Trinidad, Colorado

1985

Museum of New Mexico, Neg. No. 13191

Tallis (prayer shawl)

n.d.

On loan from Frank Wechter, Albuquerque

Prayer shawls are worn by Orthodox Jewish men during prayer. The corner fringes, tzitzit, are knotted in accordance with Biblical prescription. This tallis was used in New Mexico.

Traditionally, Orthodox Jewish men wear a sort of undershirt called a tallis katan (small tallis), which has a tzitzit on each corner. While the tallis katan is worn under garments, the tzitzit are untucked and worn in the open. In the modern age the daily tallis has been replaced by a prayer shawl (also called a tallis), worn during morning and afternoon services.

The prayer shawl shown here has a tzitzit on each corner, and a collar piece, called an atarah. The atarah serves two general purposes: It often has on it the prayer that is recited before the tallis is put on, and it provides an orientation for wearing the tallis properly. The tzitzit is meant to be a reminder to live by the laws of the Torah, not the desires of humanity. It is worn during the day because the Torah commands, "that you may see it." The tzitzit is specially knotted fringe, whose construction is full of symbolism. It is made of eight strands of string (one longer than the others) with meaningful wraps and knots. The windings state that God is one. The numerical significance of the word tzitzit, added to the number of knots, plus the number of strands, equals 613, the number of commandments listed in the Torah.

Bible

1870s

The Herzstein Family Bible.

On loan from the Union County Historical Society/
Herzstein Memorial Museum

Star of David, Las Vegas Cemetery

Photograph by Cary Herz, Albuquerque. Used by permission.

The Tetragrammaton

Above the entrance to St. Francis Cathedral are the four consonants of the ancient Hebrew name for God—known as the Tetragrammaton—inscribed within a triangle, a common Christian symbol for the Trinity. It remains a mystery whether Archbishop Jean Baptiste Lamy intended this simply as a traditional Christian symbol, or if he had the inscription added specifically to honor his friendship with the Jewish community of Santa Fe, which contributed generously to the construction of the cathedral.

According to Elizabeth Nordhaus Minces, "In 1967 Grandfather Staab was posthumously honored at the Annual Conference of Christians and Jews for his help in building the Cathedral in Santa Fe. On three different occasions Grandfather loaned money to construct the church. When the mortgage came due, the Archbishop announced sadly that he could not repay the loan. Grandfather tore up the papers, and in gratitude, the Archbishop put the Hebrew inscription on the door of the cathedral and there you will find it when you go to Santa Fe.

—Elizabeth Nordhaus Minces,
The Family: Early Days in New Mexico

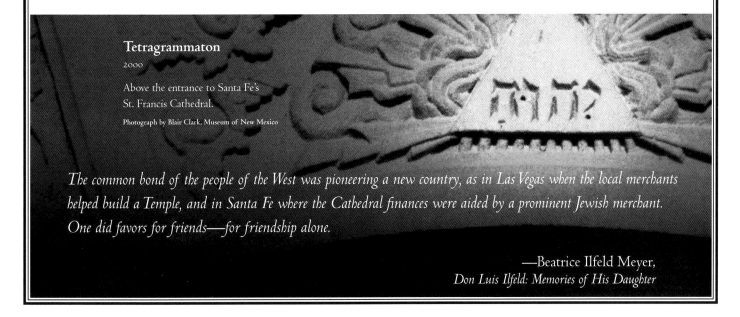

Tetragrammaton
2000

Above the entrance to Santa Fe's
St. Francis Cathedral.

Photograph by Blair Clark, Museum of New Mexico

The common bond of the people of the West was pioneering a new country, as in Las Vegas when the local merchants helped build a Temple, and in Santa Fe where the Cathedral finances were aided by a prominent Jewish merchant. One did favors for friends—for friendship alone.

—Beatrice Ilfeld Meyer,
Don Luis Ilfeld: Memories of His Daughter

Grave Marker
Montefiore Cemetery, Las Vegas
2000
Photograph by Blair Clark, Museum of New Mexico

We can readily appreciate that in the life of each of these isolated Jews there must be a story of infinite human interest, a romance of tears and laughter, adversities and triumphs.

—Sara Grant, March 4, 1927

Montefiore Cemetery, Las Vegas
1988

at right: Rabbi Leonard Helman of Santa Fe
conducts a prayer.

Photograph by Cary Herz, Albuquerque. Used by permission.

Phylacteries
n.d.

These two leather boxes (called *tefillin*, which means "prayer" in Hebrew), fastened to leather straps, contain four portions of the Pentateuch written on parchment. A phylactery is bound to the arm and head of a Jewish man during week-day morning prayers. There is a system, or pattern, to the wrapping, which symbolizes the oneness of God.

On loan from Morris & Ethel Bell & Family, Santa Fe

Cloth Envelope
n.d.

Used to mail the phylacteries from Lithuania to Morris Bell,

On loan from Morris and Ethel Bell and Family, Santa Fe

Afterword

The interest of Anglos, that is, non-Indian, non-Hispanic persons, in their own place in New Mexico history began with their writing of territorial histories in the late nineteenth century. In these works the Jewish citizens of historical consequence appear simply as citizens of the Territory. Interest in the history of Jewish New Mexican as Jews, however, did not begin in any significant way until the post-World War II period. By that time the "pioneer" era associated with the Santa Fe Trail had ended with the coming of the railroad in 1880. A secondary "pioneer" period, which was characterized by the growth of ranching in eastern New Mexico and the creation of railroad towns, lasted approximately to World War I. Roughly speaking, these two periods are covered in this publication. Undoubtedly, the sharp changes introduced into the state by the events of the second world war brought that earlier time into sharp relief, producing the sense of a distinct past far removed from the post-war present.

Few of those persons who had been present to 1920 committed their own lives to paper in the form of memoirs or diaries. Jewish old-timers, like their non-Jewish counterparts, were often too busy with their own affairs to evaluate their own lives or consider their historical value. It fell to later generations who developed sufficient curiosity about them to urge the remaining pioneers to commit their recollections to an establishable record.

Among those who wrote New Mexico history specifically involving Jews were such persons as William J. Parish, who wrote a classic history of the Charles Ilfeld Company but concentrated on the economic processes of its development rather than the Jewishness of the company's creator. However, Rabbi Floyd S. Fierman of El Paso and Rabbi Abraham I. Shinedling of Albuquerque altered the emphasis to an interest in the pioneer Jews themselves. With historical training at Hebrew Union College in Cincinnati, the latter two gentleman, under the guidance of Dr. Jacob R. Marcus, contributed much to the gathering and preservation of individual biographies that have allowed the record of early Jewish settlers to come to light and remain extant.

Beyond the writers of history, the pioneers' descendants themselves formed an inescapably important contingent in the process of recollection and preservation. Their forefathers having departed, some of them no longer had a direct connection with New Mexico. However, they passed on their own gathered memories and artifacts to succeeding generations, and their recollections form the heart and soul of this book and the exhibition at the Museum of New Mexico's Palace of the Governors on which it is based. Mrs. Susan Warburg, a descendant of Santa Fe's Spiegelberg family, whose forefathers include the earliest Jewish settlers in New Mexico, is a prime example of that path of remembrance. A host of other families never left New Mexico. Many of them, such as the Seligmans, associated in their youth with Bernalillo, remained part of the New Mexico Jewish community that continued to exist, and even to grow, after 1920.

Before World War I, New Mexico's Jews had always participated in the affairs of the general community. They played significant roles in the political life of the territory and state, contributed financially to important local causes, and created their own institutions in the form of religious congregations, as their numbers and inclinations permitted. Nevertheless, for the most part they were discreet about their Judaism as they assimilated into the broader population.

As it did in so many areas, World War II and its immediate aftermath introduced changes into New Mexico and its Jewish population that allowed and, indeed, insisted upon a new awareness of Jewish identity. The wartime demands of the federal government upon New Mexico's open and isolated spaces broke the considerable isolation that still remained, even after the coming of the railroad and the growth of road traffic. Air Force bases and defense industries introduced during the war expanded because of the Cold War and brought unprecedented numbers of newcomers, including Jews, to the state.

These newcomers broke the mold of entrepreneurship that heavily dominated Jewish economic life during its entire pioneer period. From their earliest arrival in the years after the war, they came as scientists and professionals, adding greatly to the variety of social and political expression among Jews in the community.

For the Jews themselves, few events of their history could match the power of what the war brought about. The Holocaust stood, and stands, as a landmark of unbelievable horror that never leaves Jewish consciousness. The creation of Israel shortly after the war represented a sign of survival and renewal. Together these events stirred a sense of community activism and a determination not to forget the past. While its incipient industries brought unprecedented numbers of Jews to New Mexico, the memories and tasks imposed by the war led them to organize themselves to a degree barely seen in New Mexico before the war.

Unlike in prewar generations, recollections of the past became an important issue in its own right. The quiet existence of that earlier time could not satisfy the needs of the new era. Aid to refugees, matters relating to Israel, and the need to address such matters publicly became part of a state of mind for Jews that involved honoring their own past.

Nor did Jews remain aloof from the new issues that confronted American society. Civil rights, not a new matter for Jews, and feminism, to which Jewish women responded with considerable fervor, helped

produce a community that was far more activist than its prewar brethren could possibly have imagined or desired. The rise of a strong multiculturalism became part of New Mexico's history, and New Mexico's Jews participated in that development.

    The awareness of a Jewish past in New Mexico grew. In the 1980s, the still relatively small community even created its own historical society. Its felt obligations included caring for cemeteries of older and nearly defunct Jewish communities, such as the one in Las Vegas that had become dilapidated.

    Nor did the relatively narrow range of religious expression established before the war remain within the old parameters. By the end of the twentieth century, Orthodoxy joined Reform and Conservative congregations and a host of religious organizations that expressed various tendencies already present elsewhere in the United States. New Mexico even became home for a congregation founded by a female rabbi, although not without difficulty. Thus, the New Mexico Jewish community began to resemble other larger American Jewish communities rather than remaining within the narrower social and economic range known pre-war.

    And in the postwar period, unique features of New Mexico's Hispanic past attracted the attention of the Jewish community. The surfacing of crypto-Judaism, a remnant of Spain's Inquisitionist past, drew awareness not only to Jews but also to the element in the Hispanic population that brought it to light. Sometimes a matter of sharp contention, that chapter of earlier Sephardic Jewish history is only beginning to be written.

Spiegelberg Family Reunion

July 17, 1988

This photograph was taken in front of the Willi Spiegelberg family home in Santa Fe.

Photography by Cary Herz, Albuquerque. Used by permission.

The growth and development of the Jewish community of New Mexico—some ninefold since the war—gradually introduced social issues that could no longer remain in the hands of small congregations. Such matters as caring for the aged, dealing with refugees, and contributing to the defense of Israel demanded a range of commitment that extended beyond loyalty to one's chosen branch of Judaic religious expression. There had to be room for those who did not belong to specific congregations and issues that could be considered secular rather than religious. A Jewish community center such as now exists in Albuquerque became a reality in the 1990s, as did Jewish education for children, whose opportunities for such enlightenment had previously rested only within the congregations themselves.

The growing tolerance and openness of American society also made themselves felt. Although intermarriage had always been a concern for some American Jews, who feared that such a path would lead to the disappearance of Jewry, new attitudes allowed the opposite possibility—that non-Jewish marriage partners could accept Judaism. In New Mexico, where paucity of Jewish numbers made the path of disappearance theoretically conceivable, such matters now had to be rethought.

The postwar increase in tolerance also affected New Mexico's Jews in other ways. Christian groups were led both by the experience of the war and the creation of Israel to reconsider their historical role of enmity toward Jews. These events inspired many to seek to interact with the Jewish community in ways that would have been unthinkable before World War II. The results of Vatican Council II in the 1960s and reforms of some Protestant groups have led to sensitivity of a high order in New Mexico and to regular interfaith dialogues readily accepted among the religions.

Old, entrenched views do not die easily. Fears of a renewal of anti-Semitism, which was never strong but nevertheless was present in New Mexico, remain. The threat of extinction persists through the very openness of American society, even though the numbers of New Mexico's Jews have grown much faster than those of the state's total population. One cannot help but wonder what the old Jewish pioneers would have thought of the Jewish communities of today's New Mexico. It is hard to imagine that they could regard them with anything but astonishment and optimism.

—Henry J. Tobias

Bibliography

Many works, published and unpublished, contributed to the exhibition as well as to this book. The major reference and most comprehensive work of Jewish history in New Mexico is Henry Tobias's *The History of Jews in New Mexico.* The New Mexico Historical Review published numerous articles about Jewish life in New Mexico. In addition to privately held material and oral information provided in interviews and elsewhere, which are quoted liberally throughout this work, the New Mexico State Records Center and Archives (Santa Fe), the Center for Southwest Research, the University of New Mexico (Albuquerque), the Fray Angélico Chávez History Library, the Palace of the Governors (Santa Fe), and the American Jewish Archives (Cincinnati, Ohio) hold major archival collections documenting the activities of Jewish pioneers in New Mexico. Below are a few major published works used for this book.

"Germantown: 300 Jahre Auswanderung in die USA, 1683–1983," *Zeitschrift fürKulturaustausch* 32, no. 4 (1982).

Fierman, Floyd S. "Nathan Bibo's Reminiscences of Early New Mexico," *El Palacio* 69 (Spring 1962): 40–59.

Meketa, Jacqueline. *Louis Felsenthal: Citizen-Soldier of Territorial New Mexico.* Albuquerque: University of New Mexico Press, 1982.

Meyer, Beatrice Ilfeld. *Don Luis Ilfeld: Memories of His Daughters.* Albuquerque: Albuquerque Historical Society, 1973.

Meyer, Marian. *Santa Fe's Fifteen Club: A Century of Literary Women.* Santa Fe: Fifteen Club, 1991.

Minces, Elizabeth Nordhaus. *The Family: Early Days in New Mexico.* Albuquerque: The Author, 1980.

Nahm, Milton C. *Las Vegas and Uncle Joe: The New Mexico I Remember.* Norman, Okla.: University of Oklahoma Press [1964].

Parish, William J. *The Charles Ilfeld Company: A Study of the Rise and Decline of Mercantile Capitalism in New Mexico.* Cambridge, MA: Harvard University Press, 1961.

Remley, David A. *Bell Ranch: Cattle Ranching in the Southwest, 1824–1947.* Albuquerque: University of New Mexico Press, 1993.

Tobias, Henry J. *The History of the Jews in New Mexico.* Albuquerque: University of New Mexico Press, 1990.

Twitchell, Ralph E. *Old Santa Fe: The Story of New Mexico's Ancient Capital.* Santa Fe: *Santa Fe New Mexican,* 1925.

Additional Suggested Readings

Cook, Mary Jean. "Flora Spiegelberg, 'Tenderfoot Bride of the Santa Fe Trail,'" *Wagon Tracks* (November 2000).

Fierman, Floyd. *Guts and Ruts: The Jewish Pioneer on the Trail in the American Southwest.* Hoboken, N.J.: KTAV Publishing House, 1985.

———. *Roots and Boots: From Crypto-Jew in New Spain to Community Leader in the American Southwest.* Hoboken, N.J.: KTAV Publishing House, 1987.

Gerber, Jane S. *The Jews of Spain: A History of the Sephardic Experience.* New York: Free Press, 1994.

Gitlitz, David M. *Secrecy and Deceit: The Religion of the Crypto-Jews.* Albuquerque: University of New Mexico Press, 2002.

Mann, Vivian B., et al., eds. *Convivencia: Jews, Muslims, and Christians in Medieval Spain.* New York: G. Braziller, 1992.

Marks, Mel. *Jews Among the Indians: Tales of Adventures and Conflict in the Old West.* Chicago: Benison Books, 1992.

Rischin, Moses, and John Livingston. *Jews of the American West.* Detroit: Wayne State University Press, 1991.

Rochlin, Harriet, and Fred Rochlin. *Pioneer Jews: A New Life in the Far West.* Boston: Houghton Mifflin, 2000.